PELICAN BOOKS

Advisory Editors : H. L. BEALES, Reader in Economic
History, University of London ; W. E. WILLIAMS,
Director, the Army Bureau of Current Affairs ;
Secretary, the British Institute of Adult Education.

BRITAIN UNDER THE ROMANS

BY

S. E. WINBOLT

(A 134)

THE AUTHOR

S. E. WINBOLT, educated at Christ's Hospital and Corpus, Oxford, returned to his school as a master in classics and history.

Seeking for tangible and visible illustrations, he spent much time in English and Continental museums—on which he gave B.B.C. talks—and began practical excavation in 1922; thereafter he excavated four Roman villas, dug two Roman posting stations, made countless sections of Roman roads, and found and dug a score of medieval glasshouse sites. Added to this, he investigated six Early Iron Age camps in Sussex, Surrey and Kent.

Included in his long list of publications are ROMAN FOLKESTONE, WITH A SPADE ON STANE STREET, two successful PENGUIN GUIDES and a *Pelican Book* (A 106) on Britain B.C., and on archæology he contributed to *The Times*, *Evening News*, *The Listener*, and other papers.

As cyclist, motorist, and hiker he covered much of Great Britain and travelled extensively in Europe.

Mr. Winbolt died in 1944.

PELICAN BOOKS

BRITAIN UNDER THE ROMANS

by

S. E. WINBOLT

PUBLISHED BY

PENGUIN BOOKS

HARMONDSWORTH MIDDLESEX ENGLAND

245 FIFTH AVENUE NEW YORK U.S.A.

First published 1945

MADE AND PRINTED IN GREAT BRITAIN FOR PENGUIN BOOKS LIMITED, BY RICHARD CLAY AND COMPANY, LTD., BUNGAY, SUFFOLK.

CONTENTS

v

PREFACE

THIS book carries on our island story from my Penguin *Britain B.C.*
As a farmer in the market displays his grain in open hand, so all
I pretend to do is to offer samples of the harvest Roman Britain
holds for student and tourist. The open country and museums
afford a stimulus in almost all districts, and the libraries contain
trustworthy books. I hope I have succeeded in conveying *multum
in parvo*, aided greatly by the writings of Haverfield, Collingwood,
Ward and dozens of others.

S. E. WINBOLT.

Horsham,
Sussex.

FIG. 1.—MAP OF ROMAN BRITAIN.
(By permission of Methuen & Co., Ltd).

BRITAIN UNDER THE ROMANS

CHAPTER I

HISTORICAL SKETCH

A. *Caesar to the Claudian Invasion* : 55 B.C.–A.D. 43. *The Princes of Camulodunum.*

GAUL pacified, Rome would sooner or later reach out for Britain. Caesar's reason for his invasion of 55 and 54 B.C. was the danger of a free Britain to Gaul, with which the island was closely connected by geographical position, by tribes, and by a common desire for independence; the Britons had, besides, helped the Gauls in their struggle against him. Augustus (29 B.C.–A.D. 14) recognized, but circumspectly avoided this policy: Horace describes some wishful thinking in his lines, "Augustus will be held a powerful divinity when the Britons have been annexed to the Empire". But Gaul, which did not cease from troubling, stopped the way. However, the mutual jealousy and strife of the British kinglets both provided opportunities for and helped Roman invasion, just as they did the Saxon inroads four and a half centuries later. Some of the princes whose cause the Romans had espoused became their *socii* (allies), in order to maintain, as they hoped, their own independence. The dealings of the Romans with tribal chiefs are illustrated by several examples, since Caesar, in his second campaign (B.C. 54), in which Cassivellaunus was defeated, reinstated as King of the Trinovantes at Camulodunum (later Colchester), Mandubracius whose father had been killed by Cassivellaunus, prince of the Catuvellauni. This tribe were seeking to impose princes of their own dynasty on neighbouring and subject tribes; in the instance of Mandubracius' father the Trinovantes had suffered, and perhaps the chief internal dispute in southern Britain from Caesar to Claudius centred in the succession of princes at Camulodunum. For a time the Catuvellauni ceased to harry the Trinovantes, and extended their territory northwards from their new capital of Verulamium, successor to their Wheathampstead fortress. Dubnovellaunus, who appealed to Augustus, was probably the successor of Mandubracius; Adminius (Amminius) was certainly the son of Cunobelinus, who ruled at Camulodunum. Exiled by his father, he appealed to the Emperor Gaius (Caligula), who thereupon sent a message to the

Senate that Britain had been added to the Roman power! Trouble was brewing in Britain, probably because Claudius refused to give up Adminius. It is not known certainly who Bericus was, but Dio says that he was driven out of Britain in an insurrection and took refuge with Claudius, persuading him to invade the island. It may be that he was a prince of the Iceni, and that when Claudius sent the army in A.D. 43, Bericus persuaded his own supporters to enter into alliance with the Romans.

Here is a brief summary of the history. After Caesar's campaigns the Britons felt they were reasonably secure from conquest for some time to come. Commius, whom Caesar had made king of the Continental Atrebates and had sent over to Britain before his first expedition—he was in Britain during both expeditions—proved disloyal, joined Vercingetorix at Alesia, and escaped from Caesar in Gaul by sailing with a fleet and Belgic supporters to Britain about 50 B.C. Landing at or near Southampton, he penetrated Hants, where [1] later was founded Calleva Atrebatum (Silchester). These western Belgae gradually took possession of the central region of southern England, i.e., Hants, Berks, West Surrey and the chalk hills of Wessex, with a western boundary from Swindon to Bournemouth. There had been an earlier Belgic settlement of Kent and Herts and a district north of the Thames under Cassivellaunus. Coins of Commius and his sons Tincommius, Verica and Eppillus are found in Kent, Surrey, Sussex, Hants and perhaps a part of Wilts, and they suggest a divided rule over the Cantii, Regni (West Sussex) and Atrebates—Eppillus in north-east Kent, Tincommius in Sussex and Hants, and Verica round Silchester. They ruled about the early years of Augustus, towards the end of the first century B.C. Early in Augustus' reign at Verulam was ruling Tasciovanus, whose coins are numerous, mainly in Herts, Beds and Bucks, and "indicate a long and prosperous reign"; he was probably a grandson of Cassivellaunus. His sons' names, Cunobelinus and Epaticcus, also appear on coins. Cunobelinus later on made Camulodunum his capital, having probably driven thence Dubnovellaunus, who fled to Augustus. Tasciovanus lived until at least 13 B.C., and perhaps some years later.

Cunobelinus (Cymbeline) had a long reign at Camulodunum: his coins are many. He was probably established in his town late in the reign of Augustus (c. A.D. 5), and lived until about A.D. 40–43—i.e., until shortly before the Claudian invasion, in which his sons Caratacus and Togodumnus fought against the Romans. His power extended to the south coast, where he exercised some

---

[1] Probably about 1 A.D.

kind of authority over the local princes: Suetonius calls him " Rex Britannorum ". He lived through the reign of Tiberius (A.D. 14–37), who is not recorded to have had dealings with Britain; but during the reign of Gaius (A.D. 37–41), Cunobelinus banished his son Adminius, who, with a few followers, surrendered himself in Gaul to the Emperor, whose absurd boast has been mentioned. Cunobelinus dying soon after this, there followed " internal dissensions and a repudiation of Roman suzerainty ", which he had probably recognized to some extent. Other coin-minting kingdoms of the time were those of the Dobuni, round Cirencester, spreading along the Cotswolds and east to Oxford, and west over the Severn; the Brigantes of Yorks and round the Humber, spreading over Lincolnshire and Nottinghamshire, and the Iceni of East Anglia.

Claudius became emperor in A.D. 41. The Romanization of Britain before the invasion has been summed up by Haverfield. It was very considerable. Intercourse between the island and the Empire began with the conquest of Gaul by Caesar (58–51 B.C.) and continued with the Romanization of Gaul under Augustus. British coins begin to be inscribed before 30 B.C., and a little later they are found to be changing their character from the old stater type to Roman models. Roman coins of Republican date—*e.g.*, *denarii* (silver coins of about the size of a sixpence) of *c.* 100 B.C.—occur in Britain both singly and in hoards; some of them may have come in early by way of trade and remained in circulation. " Arretine " pottery—*i.e.*, Italian-made between 30 B.C. and A.D. 20 —of the Augustan and Tiberian age, was imported and freely used at Silchester (Calleva Atrebatum), where some degree of Romanization was in process long before A.D. 43. Pieces of this ware are found also at London, Colchester, Heybridge (Essex), Foxton (Cambs), Alchester and Bicester (Oxon), Purbeck (Dorset) and Oare (Wilts). Italian bronze vases and brooches were also imported. To judge by the many coins of Claudius found in the Thames on the line of old London Bridge, and by the Arretine fragments found in London and Southwark, as well as by the indications of early burials, it seems possible that Roman merchants had settled there before the troops landed in Britain, as it is certain that such settlements were made elsewhere—*e.g.*, in Gaul. Tending towards the spread of Roman influence in south-east Britain was the acceptance of Roman suzerainty by some of the British kings, especially during the long reign of Cunobelinus, who, though he did not ask for the friendship of Rome, does not appear to have been otherwise than friendly. This attitude helps to explain the considerable import of necklaces, bracelets, glass-ware, amber ornaments, etc., and the export, recorded by Strabo, of cattle, wheat, hides, slaves, hunting-dogs, and of gold, silver and iron. The number of amphorae—big two-handled wine-jars—found, means a flourishing wine trade, carried on, as with the other commodities, from London and Colchester. The excavations of 1933 on the site of the capital of Cunobelinus gave full evidence of Roman material culture.

But the acceptance of Roman products does not mean that the Celtic Britons before Claudius had no artistic products of their own. These are often " the work of accomplished artists, gifted with a sense of line that has seldom been surpassed in any school " (Colling-wood). Proof of this are the shields, helmets, horse-trappings, and engraved bronze mirrors of their wealthy aristocrats, and the better class of pottery, of which Dobunian bowls found at Glastonbury, ornamented with curved lines and spirals, are good examples.

B. *The Invasion of Claudius*, A.D. 43–47.

At last the general state of the Empire permitted invasion. Caesar's argument still held, and it was now thought that taxes raised there would make Britain a paying proposition : commercial magnates and traders settled in Britain no doubt favoured the venture. In 43 the army of invasion under Aulus Plautius, governor of Pannonia, consisted of four legions—II Augusta from Strasbourg, XIV Gemina from Mainz, XX Valeria Victrix from Cologne, and IX Hispana from Pannonia—numbering 5,600 each; total of legionaries 22,400. Added to these were auxiliaries in about equal numbers, including perhaps 8,000 Batavians; grand total of over 40,000. Temporary reinforcements brought by Claudius were a detachment of the Praetorian Guard and an elephant corps.

After some mutinous hesitation the army embarked from Gaul, apparently from Boulogne and neighbourhood, in three divisions, crossing by night in a westerly direction. Landing in east Kent at Richborough, and marching and countermarching in order to find the enemy, the Romans made for the Medway, and crossed it after severe fighting, but were checked on the Thames, where there were fords across to the Lea marshes. The check was probably staged so that the Emperor Claudius might intervene. On his arrival the Thames was re-crossed and Colchester taken. Part of the tribe of the Bodunni, subject to the Catuvellauni, and several other tribes submitted to the conquerors : the Regni of Sussex and Surrey and the Iceni of Norfolk and Suffolk became *socii* either before or soon after the invasion. Cogidubnus, who is recorded on an inscribed stone from a temple he erected at Chichester, had his kingdom increased by several towns, probably when Ostorius was governor, and remained faithful to the Roman cause for many years, *ad nostram usque memoriam,* says Tacitus, who was born *c.* A.D. 55—*i.e.,* till about A.D. 65 at least. The temple containing the inscription, the villa at Bignor, early coins in Sussex, and the Chichester–London Stane Street, made probably *c.* A.D. 70, point to Romanization of the Regni well before the end of the first century.

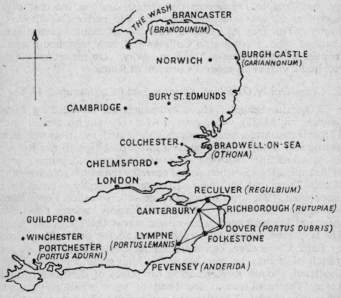

FIG. 2.—Forts of the Saxon Shore.

The subjugation of the lowlands, 44–47, seems to have been effected thus: Legio II, with auxiliaries, advanced south-westwards under Vespasian, and in that district subdued two powerful tribes, twenty fortresses, including Maiden Castle, and the Isle of Wight. Vespasian may have marched as far as Exeter: his line of advance is represented by the main roads, London–Silchester–Winchester–Southampton; Winchester–Dorchester–Exeter. Legions XIV and XX, with their auxiliaries, advanced north-westwards, probably as far as Wroxeter on the line of Watling Street, Legio IX and auxiliaries marched northwards from Colchester by Cambridge and Godmanchester. Lincoln was occupied, if not under Plautius, at any rate before the end of Claudius' reign (54). (See the line of the roads on the map.) The base whence these advances were made was the region between Colchester and London—*i.e.*, north of the Thames. The territory overrun in the first four years comprised the lowlands of S.E. Britain from the territory of the Brigantes under Queen Cartimandua round the Humber and in Derbyshire, by the Trent to the Severn (Wroxeter), and on the east of the Severn as far as Gloucester (Glevum) and perhaps south-west to Exeter. This may be gathered from the subsequent campaigns of Ostorius, who, according to Collingwood, may have had a western frontier along the line of the Fosse Way. On his return Plautius received a victorious general's ovation in Rome.

C. *Campaigns of Ostorius: Caratacus and Cartimandua, 47–58.*

P. Ostorius Scapula, whose campaigns are recorded by Tacitus (*Annals*, xii, 31–39), was governor 47–51/2. On his arrival late in 47 he found widespread disturbance caused by tribes remaining hostile and trying to stir the *socii* into opposition to the Romans. He attacked and dispersed some who resisted, adopting a policy of disarming the suspected and of coercing the whole country on this side of Trent and Severn—*i.e.*, the region already overrun by his predecessor. He drew a frontier line—the so-called Fosse Way——to defend the Dobuni and Coritani (mainly between Gloucestershire and Leicestershire) from attack across the Trent and Severn. The Fosse was drawn very straight from Seaton on the Devon coast by Bath, Cirencester, Leicester and Newark to Lincoln. A good stretch of it may be seen along the high ground north of Bath. The Iceni, though *socii*, resented the policy of disarmament, and, joining the resistance at the head of some small neighbouring tribes, gave battle. The place, an earthwork with a narrow entrance, and chosen not by the Iceni, but by their allies, was not in Icenian territory; perhaps it was in the Cambridge district, where signs of slaughter, suitable to the date, have appeared in the earthwork (War Ditches) at Cherryhinton, 3 miles south-east of Cambridge. Defeated by auxiliaries, the Iceni had to submit to disarmament, and the occupied country was for the time reduced to quiet.

In 48 and onwards Ostorius made several expeditions. One was into the country of the Degeangli (Flintshire), who were smelters of lead—new ground for the Romans. It was probably then that a fortress was established for Legs. XX and XIV at Wroxeter. Later, XX went on to Chester, but it is uncertain whether XIV went there too or was quartered at Wroxeter till its withdrawal in 67–70. Before his purpose in Flintshire was fulfilled, Ostorius had to return to quell a disturbance among the troublesome Brigantes of Yorkshire, possibly the result of a difference between a Roman and an anti-Roman party. Some understanding with this tribe had been arrived at before Ostorius, who, however, had to do some fighting before the disturbance was quelled.

In 49–50 a *colonia* of time-expired Roman soldiers was established at Camulodunum (but not fortified) as a preliminary for defence, as a reserve against hostile elements, and to help the Romanization of the *socii*; but this was done at the expense of natives dispossessed of their land. Ostorius went direct from Camulodunum against the Silures, Iberians of South Wales, who were now led by Caratacus (Caradoc), driven from the east, but accepted by the unconquered western tribes as war chief and champion of their liberties. A fortress of Leg. II which was brought up from the south was established near the fierce Silures, probably at Gloucester. Caratacus chose a rocky hill above a river in the land of the Ordovices for an advantageous fighting-place, perhaps Caer Caradoc, near Little Stretton, Salop, and with augmented forces gave battle, but was defeated by legionaries and auxiliaries. The Britons had neither breastplates nor helmets. Caratacus, whose wife, daughter and brothers were taken, himself escaped to Cartimandua, queen of the Brigantes, wife of Venutius and daughter of Volisius. But she gave him up to the Romans. Ostorius was decreed a triumph in Rome, while Caratacus, a captive in Rome, was pardoned. On his return, Ostorius had more trouble with the Silures. The *praefectus castrorum* and some cohorts of Leg. II, whose work was to build forts (*praesidia*), were surrounded, and, though help came from the nearest forts, the prefect, eight centurions and the nearest supporting legionaries were killed. Soon after, Roman foraging parties and their supports were cut off, and the legions had to be called out; but even then the Roman success was not marked. Followed a guerilla warfare in which the success of the Silures in taking spoils and prisoners encouraged others to throw off the Roman yoke. Worn out by the conflict, though not slain in battle, Ostorius died (52).

He was succeeded by A. Didius Gallus (52–57/8). Before he arrived, the Silures had worsted Leg. II under Martius Valens, and were not driven back until Didius attacked them and made the Severn Valley more defensible. Nero became emperor in 54. About the year 57 Venutius, whose brother and relatives his wife Cartimandua had treacherously killed, attacked his wife's party, and was supported by a strong force of *hostes*—probably a confederate tribe of the Brigantes. Cartimandua was pro-Roman but Venutius, who had also accepted the suzerainty and been sheltered by the arms of the Romans, turned against them, realizing that they would support his wife. Sharp fighting ensued, in which both auxiliaries and a legion, probably the IXth from Lincoln were engaged. The advance from Lincoln would be to the Humber and via Market Weighton and Stamford Bridge to York. The rising was quelled. In command was Caesius Nasica, for Didius was old and could do no more than act on the defensive against the Silures. By contrast, the next governor, D. Veranius Nepos, was energetic and determined to conquer the Silures, but he died prematurely within the year (57/8–58/9). In his will he recorded a boast, made after trifling conflicts with the Silures, that, had he lived two years longer he would have reduced the whole province of Britain for Nero.

D. *Suetonius and Boudicca; Cerialis and the Brigantes; Frontinus and the Silures, 58–78.*

C. Suetonius Paulinus, governor 58/9–61, for two years was successful, subduing tribes and establishing military stations in north Wales, with the intention of reaching the Irish Sea. It was under him that Agricola began his training, and Suetonius, appreciating his merits, chose him for work at headquarters.

His expedition to Mona (Anglesey), where many refugees from the Romans sought shelter, was in 60–61. Flat-bottomed boats were used to cross the straits, the cavalry swimming by their horses. They were opposed on the shore of the island by a large and weird host of the enemy, among whom were women fighting like Furies and encouraged by Druids. After a victorious massacre the Romans cut down the groves of human sacrifices and augury. A *praesidium* was established at Segontium (near Carnarvon), but probably abandoned immediately on the arrival of bad news: " Boudicca, at the head of a large part of the province, has raised the standard of rebellion ".

The Britons had been oppressed by both military and civil authorities; the will of Prasutagus, client king of the Iceni, who, dying in 61, had made Nero a co-heir, had been made an excuse for plundering his house by means of slaves, his kingdom by soldiers; the chiefs of the tribe, as if their inheritances were revocable gifts, had been robbed of their patrimony, and the relatives of the king had been put in bonds. The widowed Queen Boudicca and her two daughters were shamefully treated. In similar fashion the veterans of Camulodunum had plundered the native Trinovantes, treating them as captives and slaves. Roman ministers trafficking in money and financiers were ruining the British communities. Under cover of religion, the provincial priests, who presided over feasts and spectacles, were wasting the goods of the natives. What wonder that smouldering conspiracy flamed into rebellion, amid portents at Camulodunum? The unwalled *colonia* of retired legionaries was rushed and burned by Iceni and Trinovantes, the temple of Claudius, symbol of slavery, was stormed and taken in two days. In aid of a small body of soldiers on the spot Catus Decianus, the procurator (chief financial officer), had sent 200 more, not properly armed; all perished. The British host went out to meet Q. Petillius Cerialis, gallant legate of the IXth, as he was marching from Lincoln to the rescue, and overwhelmed the legion by sheer numbers, slaying all the 2000 infantry. But Cerialis and the cavalry escaped. Catus Decianus, who was chiefly responsible for the war on account of his avarice and hated by the province, got away to Gaul.

Suetonius, sending to summon Leg. II from Gloucester, by forced marches came from Anglesey through a hostile country towards the seat of war, and arrived by Watling Street at London at the head of an advanced guard of cavalry. Realizing that the place, with its merchant population and small number of soldiers, could not be defended, and learning too of Cerialis' defeat, he left London to its fate, to be sacked and burned like Colchester and Verulam: Roman citizens and *socii* were put to death by sword, fire and torture to the number of 70,000. At the beginning of the rebellion the Britons had overwhelmed some of the *castella* (small garrisoned forts), but after the sack of Camulodunum they rushed for the towns for the sake of the spoil, and neglected the *castella*. This neglect enabled Suetonius to swell his ranks with their garrisons until his army numbered about 10,000, made up of the XIVth, a detachment of the XXth which followed him from the north-west, and a considerable number of auxiliaries from the *castella* in the district where the war was raging. Now joined by his infantry, Suetonius chose his own battle-ground protected by woods in flank and rear, probably on or near Watling Street and not far from Verulam (St. Albans); and by his skilful tactics and the steady valour of his men won a great victory over the large but undisciplined hosts of the enemy. But the victory was prelude to wholesale and indiscriminate butchery, in which nearly 80,000 are said to have been killed; the Roman loss in the battle was 400 killed and slightly more wounded. The prefect of the IInd Legion, who had failed to come to the help of Suetonius, killed himself when he heard of the Roman victory.

The heroic Queen Boudicca worthily ended her noble fight for freedom by poisoning herself.

Nero now sent reinforcements—2,000 legionaries, eight cohorts of Batavian (Dutch) auxiliaries and 1,000 cavalry; the cohorts (infantry) and *alae* (cavalry) were posted to new winter quarters. Suetonius' vengeance was thorough and brutal: he carried fire and sword over the territory of the Iceni and of those who came under suspicion; and still more who, expecting to seize the Roman supplies in London, had neglected to sow crops, perished by hunger. His cruelty, and private animosity between him and Julius Classicianus, the new procurator (governor and subordinate procurator were often at loggerheads), caused the latter to spread reports that there would be no end to war until a new legate was appointed. To make enquiries Nero sent his freeman Polyclitus, who on his return gave a mild account: Classicianus held that the rebels had been punished enough. Suetonius was recalled ostensibly because he had lost a few ships. The tomb of Classicianus has been found in London.

Suetonius was succeeded (61–63) by C. Petronius Turpilianus, who, as instructed, kept the peace by his masterly inactivity: policy was being tried instead of warfare, and actually the Britons settled for a decade into some degree of contentment and prosperity. M. Trebellius Maximus Pollio (63–69) also was inactive. He fled from his army, which was idle and mutinous, and went into hiding until a sort of bargain was made, the general ruling on sufferance, while the army enjoyed its licence. Later on Roscius Caelius, legate of the XXth, rekindled the mutinous feeling against Trebellius, who made money by defrauding the soldiers of pay and equipment, and obliged him to flee from Britain. He went to Vitellius, and did not return. In 67 Nero withdrew the XIVth. After his suicide in 68, the year 69 saw four successive emperors, Galba, Otho, Vitellius and Vespasian. Vitellius sent out Vettius Bolanus (69–71) to be governor of Britain, and with him the XIVth. He, too, was for peaceful rule, but, unlike his predecessor, did not incur hatred by his misdemeanours. But disturbances continued in the army, and the trouble of a dozen years back among the Brigantes was renewed. Venutius attacked his unfaithful wife, and his tribe and certain confederates supported him. His former agreement with the Romans had now become hatred because they supported Cartimandua, and amid rumours of civil war rebellion seemed to him opportune. The Romans intervened, fighting ensued between Venutius and Roman auxiliary infantry and cavalry, and Cartimandua was rescued; but Venutius remained at the head of the

Brigantes, with the result that Rome definitely lost a (precarious) ally, and the military equilibrium of the frontier.

Agricola, appointed legate of Leg. XX, was sent (70) by Vespasian to succeed Roscius Caelius, who could not control the legions, and who, with or without excuse, had acted seditiously towards Trebellius. The XXth was apt to be too much for its legates, had a bad reputation for disobedience and rebellion, and was slow in taking the oath of allegiance to Vespasian because some of its officers had been appointed by Vitellius; indeed, the IInd was the only British legion that was quick to accept Vespasian, its leader in the war of invasion. Agricola tactfully won over the XXth, conveying the impression that he had found, rather than made them good fellows. Leg. XIV, withdrawn from Britain and returned by Nero, was finally withdrawn by Vespasian (70), and was replaced by Leg. II Adiutrix (71).

Q. Petillius Cerialis Caesius Rufus, who had been in command of Leg. IX in 61, was related to Vespasian and sent by him to be governor of Britain (71–74), after he had been fighting against Civilis (70), a Batavian chief who had raised rebellion in the Rhineland. Vespasian was set on stronger and more efficient government in Britain as in the rest of the Empire. Cerialis, or his successor Frontinus, moved the IXth from Lincoln to York in a permanent or semi-permanent camp, soon to become the principal military centre of North Britain; another camp was established at Malton. Not without much fighting and some loss, Cerialis virtually conquered a great part of Brigantia, including central and east Yorks. The Brigantes were probably a confederacy of tribes living in the whole country from sea to sea north of Trent and Humber, as far as the Tyne, and apparently as far as Birrens in Dumfries, where an inscription to " Dea Brigantia " has been found. As legate of the XXth Agricola served successfully under Cerialis, the position of the legion at Chester ensuring hard work in the northern campaigns.

A quarter of a century after Ostorius had first attacked them, the Silures (South Wales) were finally subdued by the vigorous Sextus Julius Frontinus (74–78), known not only as a soldier, but also as author of a treatise on aqueducts. After building many forts and roads, he also established garrisons among the Ordovices (central and north-west Wales, south of the Degeangli).

E. *Agricola ; Romanization of Britain and the battle of the Graupian Hill*, 78–85.

Gnaeus Julius Agricola, governor (78–85), arriving at midsummer, initiated an expedition against the Ordovices (North Wales), where Frontinus had already nearly completed the conquest of Wales. They had previously cut off an *ala* of cavalry. From H.Q. at Chester (Deva), Agricola led a detachment of legionaries and auxiliaries, and defeated the enemy in their hill country with severe loss. His attack on Mona (Anglesey) was equally successful, for the island was surrendered by the natives. Segontium, the fort near Carnarvon, was then built, or, if the first occupation dates from Suetonius seventeen years earlier, re-occupied.

Agricola now introduced reforms in his official establishment and in the administration of the province, the army was well governed and the natives treated justly, especially as regards their contributions of grain and money payments of tribute. Next year he led an expedition from Chester to the north, by the lowlands between the hills of Lancashire and the sea, passing the estuaries of Lancashire and Cumberland. Attacking with great vigour, he also made peace and submission attractive. When subdued, the tribes were surrounded by forts—*e.g.*, at Carlisle, Hardknot, Ravenglass, and Nether Denton and Corbridge on the Stanegate, a frontier road made from Carlisle to Corbridge.

Romanization. The winter was spent in the Romanization of the province. Agricola encouraged and urged the building of temples, market-places (*fora*) and houses, and also the learning of Latin. By tactfully praising the talent of the Britons, he persuaded the young native chieftains to begin to learn Latin, which they had hitherto boycotted, and to adopt the Roman dress. But in the wake of Roman amenities came Roman luxury and vices, excessive use of baths, idling in porticoes and sumptuous feasts. Romanization, of course, had already begun some century and a quarter before Agricola, but he gave a special and deliberate fillip to the movement. The Roman town-planning of Caerwent and of the previously existing Silchester may be attributed to his influence coins and pottery show that town life grew apace in the Flavian period (*i.e.*, the reigns of Vespasian, Titus and Domitian, 69–96 at Wroxeter; and the walls and fine Balkerne Gate, and possibly the town-planning of Colchester, may also be dated about this time or at least between 61 and 90. The temple at Chichester and the villa at Bignor both seem to be of Flavian date. With regard to Latin there is evidence of a teacher of rhetoric at York in Agricola's

time, one Demetrius, a Greek; Statius (*c.* 95) refers to the change
from a military to a civil condition in central Britain; Martial says
(96) that his verses were recited in Britain; Juvenal mentions (128)
British pleaders trained by Gallic eloquence; and *legati iuridici*
(pleaders in law-courts) appear in Britain soon after 80. In time
also British workmen spoke Latin, as is proved by *graffiti* on tiles
and walls. There is little doubt that the upper and lower classes
of the towns and country houses of lowland Britain became
Romanized in language as well as in their mode of living, though
in the military districts such as Northumberland and the north
the natives, except the *vicani*, who lived close to and dependent
on the forts, probably spoke little Latin.

In 80 Agricola opened up tribes hitherto unknown, laying their
territory waste as far as the Tanaus (? the Tyne). His advance,
made in bad weather, was not opposed, and he had time to make
forts of timber and earthwork, the sites for which were chosen with
skill; these forts may have included High Rochester (Bremenium),
Cappuck near Jedburgh and Newstead (Trimontium), which may
be dated about this time. The advance would have been from
York, now the military capital, by the line of the Roman road
(Leeming Lane) to Catterick and Corbridge, and on by Dere Street,
on which are the " Agricolan " forts above mentioned. The forts
established were provisioned for a year or even two years, so that
they could be held through one or two winters and be self-supporting.
From such forts excursions were often made, and the enemy,
so frequently checked, had his powers of resistance lowered.

In 81 (Domitian emperor) the territory overrun in the previous
year was secured, by the making of forts and roads. Whether
or not a considerable advance was made northwards, forts were
built between Clyde and Forth, in order that there might be a barrier
between the tribes already overpowered to the south of the isthmus
and the unconquered peoples of Caledonia. These forts were
afterwards incorporated in the forts of the Antonine Wall, built
sixty years later, or rather some of the Antonine were built over the
sites of Agricolan forts. Six of these have been recognized by the
results of excavations—Cadder, Bar Hill, Castle Cary, Rough
Castle, Camelon and Mumrills. With the exception of Camelon,
which was on the line of advance into Caledonia, these forts were
abandoned in a year or two, when Agricola adopted a new line
running north and south between the Caledonian hills and the east
coast of Scotland, along the easier ground towards the Tay and
beyond.

The campaign of the fifth year (82) is obscure. It began with a crossing of the sea (? Solway Firth), and new tribes were conquered in many battles (? in Dumfriesshire). Some forts were garrisoned in the part of Britain facing Ireland, probably in Cumberland, where some of the forts mentioned above—*e.g.*, Ravenglass (Clanoventa) on the coast and Ellenborough (Uxellodunum)—may have been established. Ireland was known to Roman merchants in Tacitus' time, and indeed it was known for its export of gold articles to the Continent in the Bronze Age. Agricola harboured an exiled Irish prince in the hope of using him in an invasion of Ireland, as British refugees were harboured by Augustus and his successors. He calculated that Ireland could be conquered by one legion and auxiliaries, say 10,000 men in all. The project never matured.

Agricola began his campaign (83) north of the Forth by searching the harbours on the east coast of Scotland with his fleet, the *Classis Britannica*, whose main function was patrolling the English Channel from Boulogne (Gessoriacum), Dover, Lympne and other ports. Previously employed for transport and supply, Agricola was the first to see it as a fighting force to terrify the natives, make raids, plunder the country and provision the army. The sailors landed, and often joined the soldiers in their camps, the two arms fraternizing, sharing provisions and yarning successes gained by army and fleet. There was a general movement of all the Caledonian tribes to oppose the Roman advance, the line of which from Camelon northwards is probably represented by the Roman road traceable by Stirling, Ardoch and Gask towards Perth and Inchtuthill on the Tay. When the Caledonians took the offensive and attacked a fort, some of the less bold of Agricola's officers counselled retreat south of the Forth; but the general ordered an advance, first dividing his army into three divisions, in order to avoid the danger of being surrounded by the much larger forces of the enemy, who also knew the country. The Caledonians at once changed their tactics, and attacked the IXth Legion, by much the weakest of the three divisions, in its camp by night, killing the sentries and breaking into the camp, where fighting took place. On the information of his scouts, Agricola sent his swiftest horse and foot in relief, so that by morning the standards of the legions shone in the light. Even then there was fierce fighting in the very gates of the camp, but the Caledonians were driven back, and would have been utterly broken had they not escaped through the marshes and woods. Roman ardour was increased by the result—the whole of Caledonia, they said, was to be invaded and conquered. Their partial success encouraged the Caledonians also, who prepared for further resistance by arming their available men, by removing women and children to safe places by consolidating the federacy of the tribes, and by councils and religious rites. But the final struggle did not take place until the following year.

At the beginning of the summer (84) Agricola lost his son, born the year before, the second lost in infancy; he had given his daughter in marriage to Tacitus just before he was appointed governor of Britain. The year's campaign was begun by a similar use of the fleet, which searched and raided the east coast of Scotland, north of the Forth. Then the army began its advance, without heavy baggage; enrolled in existing cohorts, Britons from the pacified parts of the province formed part of the army, which by rapid advance arrived at Mons Graupius, a site not yet identified, but far away from any place yet known to the Romans—Collingwood thinks the north-east part of Strathmore. It was already occupied by the enemy, numbering over 30,000 and still increasing, and commanded by Calgacus in virtue of his valour and rank. The Britons had at length put aside mutual discord and factions, and learned to combine in face of a common enemy. Speeches are attributed by Tacitus to Calgacus and Agricola. In the battle the auxiliaries, 8,000 in number, formed the Roman front, and 3,000 cavalry the wings. The legions (? three) were in reserve in front of the camp. The British army was partly on the slopes, partly on the plain with the chariots. Agricola, having extended his line for fear of envelopment, dismounted and stood before the standards of the auxiliaries. The combat began at long range, the Britons having the advantage in the number of their projectiles. At Agricola's command four cohorts of Batavians (probably raised after 70) and two of Tungrians brought the fighting to the sword-point, so gaining an advantage, the huge pointless swords and small shields of the Britons being unwieldy at close quarters. A retreat up the slopes begins; fresh Roman cohorts and the cavalry join in the fray; the British chariots are dispersed. But the great numbers of the British, who held their ground on the slopes, together with the crowding together of Roman infantry and cavalry, were unfavourable to the latter. The Britons in the rear, moving down the slopes, now tried to envelop their enemy. To counter this movement, Agricola sent four *alae* of cavalry, and it was their charge which decided the issue of the battle, first by scattering those who were trying to envelop, and then by attacking the flank and rear of the Britons. Rout and slaughter followed. The Roman pursuit was so keen that some got into difficulties in the woods, and Agricola had to send swift cohorts to rescue them. The pursuit ended only with night, and next morning Roman scouts reported the neighbourhood deserted. Of the enemy about 10,000 were killed, while the Roman loss was put at 360, including Aulus Atticus, a cohort prefect.

The summer ended, Agricola led his army back through the territory of the Boresti (? Northerners), taking hostages from them, proceeded by slow marches through the territory of the " new tribes ", that the sight of his troops might overawe them, and so returned to winter quarters. He also commanded his admiral to sail round Britain; this was done, the fleet sailing from the Portus Trucculensis (perhaps Cramond on the south shore of the Forth), round the east shore of Scotland, doubling Cape Wrath and returning by the way it had come to the port whence it had set out—i.e., it sailed round the north extremities of Britain; proving that it was really an island, as stated by Caesar, Strabo and others, but not circumnavigating the whole of Britain.

In 85 Agricola was recalled by Domitian, and Legio II Adiutrix was brought back for the Emperor's wars on the Danube. After this time only three legions, instead of four, were quartered in Britain. Troops were certainly needed on the Danube frontier, where the Romans were defeated in 85 and 86, but the opportunity for the complete subjugation of Britain, which may have seemed well within sight under Agricola, was neglected. Agricola was recalled after an exceptionally long governorship of seven years. Tacitus alleges that Domitian from jealousy acted meanly towards Agricola and had him poisoned. The final chapters of the biography Tacitus brings to a close with a splendid epilogue on the worthy commemoration of famous men.

F. *Recall of Agricola to Hadrian. Unrest in the North ;* 85–121.

Central and south Scotland, conquered by Agricola, was held for thirty or forty years after his recall, but not undisputed: Newstead was rebuilt at least once, Camelon, Ardoch and Inchtuthill probably more often during that period. It is probable, says Dr. Macdonald, that the Romans did not retire behind the Cheviots until the " great upheaval " at the end of Trajan's (89–117) or the beginning of Hadrian's (117–138) reign. The period of thirty-two years from Agricola till *c.* 117 is obscure, but there are sidelights on it showing that the military tenure of the country south of Scotland was to a certain extent progressive. For example, by *c.* 100 a *censitor*—an officer for enrolling natives in the army— was appointed at Brough (Anavio) in Derbyshire, and Agricola's road between Carlisle and Corbridge was further fortified, the small forts at Throp and Haltwhistle Burn being added to the line c. 110. The great upheaval occurred c. 117—118: there was a rising of the natives over the whole of the north or military part of the province. The Agricolan forts in Scotland, stormed by the Caledonian tribes, were abandoned, and the rebellion of the Brigantes (? under Arviragus) was more serious still, as it seems clear that they cut to pieces the unfortunate IXth stationed at York (119–120). The Roman armies retreated behind the Cheviots, not advancing again into central Scotland before the reign of Antoninus Pius (138–161), some thirty years later.

G. *Hadrian in Britain, and Hadrian's Wall :* 121–138.

Hadrian came to Britain in 121–122, but does not appear to have stayed many months, during which time, however, he put many things in order, and initiated the scheme that developed into a Wall. Leg. VI Victrix from Castra Vetera on the lower Rhine took the place of Leg. IX at York, possibly coming by sea direct from Germany to Newcastle about 120, to serve in the troubled district. At York henceforth it remained till the end of the Roman occupation. Hadrian also brought or sent under T. Pontius Sabinus *vexillationes milliariae—i.e.*, detachments of 1,000 men of legions VII Gemina, VIII Augusta and XXII Primigenia, and probably several cohorts of auxiliaries for the purpose of fortifying and pacifying Britain. Many coins with types " Address to Soldiers " and " Britannia Taken " commemorate the visit of Hadrian and of the Exercitus Britannicus.

Hadrian's policy was that of consolidation and organization, not like Trajan's, one of conquest. The insurrections quelled, he caused to be made a boundary (*limes*) to the province, to mark off Roman from barbarian territory. The standard Roman frontier of the time consisted of a road with forts and signal-towers along it, and an earthwork in front where necessary. For Hadrian's boundary the line of Agricola's Stanegate, certainly occupied and fortified in Trajan's reign, was chosen, but was greatly extended and fortified throughout its length. The fortification of the *limes* was done in stages, one succeeding another as necessary, each in addition to, but not part of, the original design. These stages were :—

    (i) A chain of forts was built from Burgh-by-Sands to Newcastle, two of which, Carvoran (Magnae) and Chesterholm (Vindolanda), were on the Stanegate ; twelve others were in front (north) of it. South of the twelve was the *limes* (*i.e.*, the *vallum*), an earthwork consisting of a broad, deep, flat-bottomed ditch, with the upcast made into mounds on either side, the whole being 100–150 ft. across. The garrisons of the forts numbered about 7,000 auxiliaries, whose work was to patrol the *limes*.

(ii) This force proving insufficient, some of the forts—*e.g.*, Birdoswald and Chesters—were enlarged, so as to hold a *cohors milliaria* (1,000 strong).

(iii) Even this was found inadequate, so there was built the Stone Wall (stone at the east, but of turves at the west end), with its milecastles and turrets, joining the forts (except three which were left to the south of it), and extending from sea to sea, from Bowness to Wallsend, two new forts being added at the west and one at the east end to prolong the defensive line. The whole work of *vallum*, forts and wall, with its changes of design, must have been carried out within the seven years 120–127. Numerous inscriptions record the work of the three legions, II, VI and XX, in building the wall. Press-gangs may have been employed under legionary officers. Inscriptions in the milecastles witness that the work was done under Aulus Platorius. The older forts, Nether Denton, Haltwhistle Burn and Throp, and probably others of Agricolan and Trajanic date, were abandoned when the newer forts and the Wall were built. For details of the Wall see below, Chap. II.

There were also outlying forts north of the Wall, which were included in Hadrian's defence system—*e.g.*, Birrens (Blatobulgium) in Dumfriesshire, Bewcastle, a few miles north of Birdoswald on the Wall, and High Rochester (Bremenium) on Dere Street. In the British section of the Antonine Itinerary, now supposed to date *c.* 125–143, Birrens, Netherby and High Rochester appear. The fortification of the *limes* was accompanied by a regrouping of the Roman troops in north Britain—*e.g.*, Nether Denton, Hardknot in Cumberland, Castleshaw and Slack in Yorks—and other forts were evacuated *c.* 120–125, their garrisons and those of Welsh forts being transferred to the Wall. Hadrian was a great builder, and many of his works remain in the provinces he visited assiduously, as well as in Rome itself. " Wherever he went Hadrian left his mark. . . . But nowhere has he left a more impressive monument than in Britain " (Collingwood). Perhaps the fine head of the Emperor found in the Thames at London (Plate I) may be a memorial of some public work he had done in the largest and wealthiest town of the province.

H. *The Reign of Antoninus Pius. The Antonine Wall :* 138–180.

Antoninus Pius (138–161) advanced, or rather doubled, the Roman frontier in Britain. The forts north of Cheviot and in central Scotland—*e.g.*, Newstead, Camelon and Ardoch—were reoccupied, and others north of Hadrian's Wall already held were retained; also Agricola's line of fortification between Forth and Clyde was adopted and fortified by a continuous wall of turf from sea to sea, linking together a series of new forts, some at least on the sites of the older ones. The object of this doubling of the frontier is not clear. According to Haverfield, it was presumably to provide another barrier outside the still-occupied Hadrian's Wall, thus increasing the difficulty of barbarian invasion by a double line; but Colling-wood suggests that the object was rather to isolate semi-hostile districts, where new hill-forts had been built, from each other, "not to keep enemies out, but to keep subjects in". Perhaps a sort of protectorate was established over the tribes between the two walls. In any case, the Antonine Wall was a temporary measure.

It was built under Lollius Urbicus in 142. It stretched 36½ miles between Bridgeness on the Forth and Old Kilpatrick on the Clyde, and was made of turves faced with clay and based on a spread of stone, 14 ft. wide, but of clay only at the east end. It was far cheaper and much less efficient than Hadrian's Wall, and its flanks were unprotected. It was the work of the three legions which had built Hadrian's Wall—namely, II, VI and XX. The V-shaped ditch on the north side of the wall is generally 40 ft. wide and 12 ft. deep, and has an outer mound on its north lip made of the upcast from the ditch. Along its south side is the military way. There were nineteen forts, never so far as 3 miles apart, and varying in size from 6½ acres (Mumrills) to 1–2 acres; there were no milecastles and turrets. As on Hadrian's Wall, the garrisons were of auxiliaries and drafts from legions, say 6,000 to 7,000 men. The Antonine Wall was occupied for about forty-two years (143–185), when, after two temporary abandonments, it was finally given up.[1]

In 154–155 C. Julius Verus, the Governor, had to suppress a rising of the Brigantes which spread over the country from Brough (Anavio) in Derbyshire to Newcastle (Pons Aelii) and north-west to Birrens (Blatobulgium) in Dumfries, beyond Hadrian's Wall; the Roman garrisons had been weakened by withdrawals of men to the Antonine Wall, one of the two temporary abandonments of which may have been caused by this rising, the other occurring

[1] *The Roman Wall in Scotland.* Sir George Macdonald.

when Sextus Calpurnius Agricola was sent (162) by Marcus Aurelius
(161–180) to quell a disturbance. This Emperor deported conquered Sarmatians, who lived between the Baltic and Caspian Seas,
to Britain, where some formed a cavalry regiment found stationed
at Ribchester in the mid-3rd century.

I. *The Great Disturbance under Commodus, and Severus' Campaigns
   and Work in the North :* 180–211.

In 181 troubles began in Britain which did not really end until the
visit of Severus twenty-seven years later. " Hitherto the initiative
had lain with Rome. Henceforth it lay with her enemies." First
came a great disaster when invading northern tribes stormed the
Antonine Wall and did much damage, killing a certain general
and destroying his forces; whereupon Commodus (180–192) sent
against them Ulpius Marcellus, " a hard man " who had already
been Governor of Britain. This invasion resulted a little later,
perhaps after a repair, in the permanent loss of the Antonine Wall,
probably evacuated by Marcellus in an orderly way, and of all the
forts in central and south Scotland—Ardoch, Camelon and Newstead; Birrens also was abandoned and never reoccupied. Roman
armies ceased to occupy any forts north of the Cheviots after this
date. For the time being Marcellus was successful in checking the
barbarians (184), and though much damage was done to the southern
wall, he maintained it. On the strength of Marcellus' success,
Commodus took the title Britannicus, the first emperor to do so.
After the departure of Marcellus, with his Draconian discipline,
came a mutiny of the army in Britain, and the murder (185) of
Perennis, the Pretorian prefect sent to quell it; and it was not
suppressed until *c.* 187, under a new legate, Pertinax, who had risen
from the lower orders by his merits.

After the death of Commodus came a struggle for the Empire.
Pertinax was chosen by the Pretorian Guard, but all three of the
claimants—the other two being Didius Julianus and Pescennius
Niger—perished in 193–194. Septimius Severus was not established as sole emperor until the defeat and suicide of Albinus in
Gaul (197). D. Clodius Septimius Albinus, appointed Governor
of Britain by Commodus and, as a stop-gap measure, made Caesar
by Severus, had taken the legions to Gaul and assumed the title of
Augustus. This withdrawal naturally invited Caledonian invasion,
and there was a wholesale wrecking of Hadrian's Wall in forts,
milecastles and turrets, which destruction was carried as far south
as York and Chester. During the early years of Severus' reign

(193–211), when he had recovered the province from Albinus, the Caledonians broke their promise not to interfere with Roman subjects and, resting on the support of their southern neighbours, the Maeatae near Hadrian's Wall, compelled the Governor, Virius Lupus, to ransom captive Romans with large sums. Severus without doubt did much work, through Lupus and other governors, in restoring (197–208) Hadrian's Wall, work made necessary by the damage done by the barbarians (181–184), but not finished in his lifetime. The " second floors " in the forts and milecastles must be attributed to him or his immediate successors. So extensive were the repairs of Severus' reign that by certain historians he came to be regarded as the original builder of the Wall.

In 208 Severus came with a very large army to carry out a great punitive expedition against the Caledonians of Perthshire and Inverness-shire. He made a new military base at Corbridge on Tyne, and at Cramond on the Firth of Forth a naval base, and thence marched through the counties of Fife, Kinross and Kincardine. Possibly he went through Forfarshire and as far as Aberdeenshire : the large expeditionary camps still to be seen between the hills and the sea on the east coast are possibly relics of his campaign—e.g., Grassy Walls, Battle Dykes and Raedykes. The Caledonians refused open battle, but their guerilla tactics cost him a great number of men. The Caledonians and Maeatae were kept quiet for only a short spell : they were soon in arms again when Severus was at York (Eburacum), his headquarters and the military capital, probably since Agricola, with a *palatium*.

Apart from the Wall, it is likely that Severus did other building in Britain—e.g., the walls of Chester and, according to Dr. R. E. M. Wheeler's excavations, the stone walls at Carnarvon (Segontium) : some work there was certainly his. Severus was already sixty-two years old when he came to Britain, and was in bad health ; but, though he had to be carried in a litter through his expeditions, his energy and determination in campaigning, building, clearing woods and making roads and bridges were remarkable. He died at York in 211, where his body was cremated, the ashes being taken to Rome. His sons Antoninus (Caracalla) and Geta immediately withdrew the garrisons from the regions their father had wrested from the enemy, and returned to Rome. No territory, then, was permanently regained by Severus' laborious and costly expeditions, but by inflicting heavy loss on the enemy he taught them a severe lesson, and the Hadrianic frontier had henceforth nearly a century of peace.

As a result of the struggle for empire of Severus with Albinus,

the governorship of Britain was divided (197), and two provinces
—Upper and Lower Britain—were formed. The probable motive
of the division was that one governor should not have the whole
army under his control, so that it would be less easy for him to repeat
the challenge of Albinus. It is uncertain where was the boundary
between the two provinces. Inscriptions show that the change was
made under Severus, that York and the Wall (one legion and most
of the auxiliaries) were in Britannia Inferior, that Chester and
Caerleon (*i.e.*, two legions) were in Britannia Superior, and that
Lincoln was in Inferior. In the north the boundary seems to have
run through north-west Yorks. Governors mentioned after the
division were perhaps " governors of the larger province of Britannia
Superior, exercising at need a general control of the whole Roman
area " (Atkinson).

J. *Death of Severus to Carausius' Usurpation. Increased Prosperity of Britain :* 211–286/7.

For the next seventy-five years written history almost fails us,
but archaeology helps to fill the gap. Taken as a whole, the 3rd
century in Britain, in spite of its own difficulties and setbacks, was
one of comparative peace and prosperity, standing out against a
rather sombre Continental background of troubles from invasions
of the Empire. Thus there were constant inroads of barbarians
on Danube and Rhine; the Franks crossed the lower Rhine, over-
flowed all Gaul, penetrated Spain and pillaged the coast of Africa;
for nearly ten years (265–275) the Alemanni ravaged Upper Italy;
the Burgundians advanced as far west as the Upper Main; and it
was not until the close of the century and onwards, under the
Emperors Diocletian, Constantius Chlorus and Constantine the
Great, that the invading barbarians were kept " within measured
bounds ". Archaeology suggests that the state of Britain was
more settled.

In the military area inscriptions containing the names of several
emperors during fifty years record work done in fortresses from
Caerleon in the south to the Wall and beyond. Rebuilding or
restoration of headquarters (*principia*), armouries (*armamentaria*),
soldiers' barracks (*centuriae*), baths, basilicas and temples are recorded. Coins and pottery also show full occupation of certain
forts (*e.g.*, Segontium by Carnarvon) from Severus onwards.
The army seems to have held its positions, but after the middle of
the 3rd century, inscriptions in Britain become rare, and during
the last quarter almost entirely cease, except on milestones. Some

time in the century Astorius Justus, commander of the VIth, was sent with legionary cohorts and *alae* to quell a revolt in Armorica (Brittany).

In the civil area, towns which even in the south had certainly in some way felt the effect of the troubles of the end of the 2nd and beginning of the 3rd centuries, began to build or add to their walls. The walls of Aldborough (Isurium) in Yorks probably belong to the latter half of the 2nd century, the stone walls added to the earlier banks of Caerwent (Venta Silurum) and those of Silchester to the 3rd century. With greater peace the prosperity of Britain increased, country houses and farms multiplied. Large country houses such as Bignor, North Leigh and Folkestone were earlier, and houses and farms of the 1st century onwards have been found in the south (*e.g.*, in Kent), but in the 3rd they became common all over the civilized area. Britain reached its highest point of material prosperity in the Constantinian age.

There were, however, difficulties and setbacks from invasions of barbarians: there must have been a northern raid some time after 270 which drove the garrison from Hadrian's Wall. About the same time the Saxons and the Franks from Schleswig-Holstein about the Lower Elbe began to attack the coasts of Gaul and of Britain. The coin-hoards found in Britain, which were deposited shortly or immediately before Carausius (*c.* 280–285), probably witness to the disturbances in north and south: the five hoards, all of this period, found near Eastbourne point clearly to the Saxon raids.

K. *Carausius and Allectus :* 286(7)–296.

In the last quarter of the 3rd century the troubles to Gaul and Britain from the Saxon, Frankish and possibly Scandinavian pirates became so acute that active measures for the protection of both coasts were taken. M. Aurelius Mausaeus Carausius was a native of Menapia, a district about the mouths of Rhine and Meuse. He had risen from the ranks, but was an able and experienced seaman, and evidently a naval officer who had distinguished himself in war. He was given command of the Channel Fleet (*Classis Britannica*) with the purpose of keeping clear the sea washing the coasts of Belgium and Armorica (Brittany). The opposite coast of Britain also, we may suppose, needed defence against the crews of Saxon keels that put into the harbours to harry and kill, as far west as Southampton Water. The fleet, with headquarters at Boulogne (Gessoriacum), and subsidiary stations along the coasts, was to undertake an extended patrol to meet the present danger. Carausius caught the German pirates and wrested from them much booty, which he was accused of keeping instead of sending it to the Imperial treasury. He was further suspected of enriching himself by compounding with the enemy, with the result that Maximian, Diocletian's colleague as Caesar, ordered that he should be killed. Carausius, however, at the head of a large fleet, obtained also the suffrages of the army in Britain and assumed the purple, becoming the emperor of a Roman–British empire (as Postumus some twenty-seven years before had become a Roman-Gallic emperor), but not the champion of British home-rule. The " coup " of Carausius was made c. 286(7), and although efforts were made by the Roman forces to invade Britain—Constantius besieging Boulogne and beginning to build fresh ships in place of those that had followed Carausius—no headway could be made against the usurper, and the emperor Diocletian (284–305) and Maximian, his colleague as Caesar since 286, were obliged to come to terms and to recognize his authority with the title of Augustus as one of the trio—till they should be able to do otherwise.

Carausius seems to have ruled Britain strongly and prosperously for seven years. Increasing his fleet and manning it with foreign mercenaries as a strong bulwark against the invasion the Romans planned but could not effect, he was then free to devote his attention to the internal affairs of his " empire ". The number of coins struck during his reign—his chief mint was at London—witnesses to continuing commerce. He did some work at the Wall, probably restoring or partly restoring the damage done by the Northern tribes in 275.

In 294 Carausius was murdered by Allectus, one of his own officers, who aspired to and seized the " British Empire ". He was not so strong as Carausius. Two years later (296) the Imperial Government undertook and carried out the reconquest of Britain. Constantius Chlorus, then Caesar and in command of Cisalpine Gaul, sailed across the Channel from Boulogne and Havre with a large fleet, the main section of which eluded Allectus' fleet in a mist, and reached the south coast near the Isle of Wight, where Asclepiodotus, the general, landed and made contact with Allectus inland. The battle, probably at or near Woolmer in north-east Hants (where a hoard of 30,000 coins, part of the army pay-chest, was found), was decisive: Allectus and many of his men were killed, and resistance crushed. Some of his Frankish soldiers, escaping from the defeat, fled to London, spoiled the city and were about to return home, when Constantius, who with part of the fleet had been hindered by the mist and had coasted round by Richborough and up the Thames, arrived in London. He slew the Franks in the streets and recovered the spoils. A fine gold medallion of Constantius found near Arras (1922) commemorates the welcome of London to her deliverers: the city personified kneels at the gate and holds out her hands to Constantius riding on horseback, while below on the river is a boat with soldiers. The legend is ' Redditor Lucis Aeternae '—Restorer of the eternal light (of Roman civilisation).

L. *Constantius, Constantine I and his Age :* 296–337.

After the defeat of Allectus and the restoration of Britain to the Empire, Constantius (296–306) made his headquarters at York, where he rebuilt the fortress (*e.g.*, the " multangular tower "), and whence he set out (306) on his campaigns against the Picts and Irish (Hiberni or Scotti). The name " Picts " (Lat. *Picti*, painted or tattooed men) as first used was not strictly an ethnological name. The Picts may have been the same as the Maeatae (above): the Irish (Scotti) had begun to migrate into Britain in the 2nd century, making their settlements in Galloway and Argyll, whence, and from Ireland also, they began to raid the whole west coast of England and Wales. Constantius may have gone beyond the Wall in his latest expedition in order to check the Picts and leave the Wall more secure. By rebuilding Wall defences he put the frontier once more in order. In the south he restored the walls of Verulam, at least. He died at York (306), his son Constantine arriving just in time to receive his father's last embrace. The funeral was at York, where Constantine assumed the title of Caesar and was proclaimed Emperor.

The reign and age of Constantine, including also a few years before he was actually emperor while Diocletian was still reigning, brought great changes to Britain as part of the Roman Empire. Of these, two were the reorganization of the army and the peace of the Church. In Britain are found two new military officials, the Dux Britanniarum and the Comes Litoris Saxonici (Count of the Saxon Shore). The Dux had his command at York, his forces being stationed round York, on the Wall and along the Cumberland coast, etc., all in the north, where Picts and Scots needed restraint. The Comes had to defend, as his title implies, the shore that was attacked by Saxon pirates. This shore had been defended from the sea by the Fleet (*Classis Britannica*), but after the exploits of Carausius and the recovery of Britain from Allectus, the Imperial authority

B   (A 134)

changed the mode of defence. Nine or ten forts were established, almost certainly by Constantius, along the shore from the Wash to Portsmouth Harbour, all of the later type, with thick walls and external bastions, each fort built right down to the water's edge so that ships could come to its gates, a fact which showed that it was a port as well as a fort, a base for a naval coast patrol. The *Notitia Dignitatum*, an official list dating *c.* A.D. 428 and incorporating a list of much earlier date, mentions nine, here arranged in geographical order from Norfolk round the coast to Hants: 1. Branodunum (Brancaster), 2. Gariannonum (Burgh Castle), 3. Othona (Bradwell), 4. Regulbium (Reculver), 5. Rutupiae (Richborough), 6. Dubrae (Dover), 7. Lemanis (Lympne), 8. Anderida (Pevensey), 9. Portus Adurni (Portchester). To these may be added 10. Carisbrooke, I.o.W. These forts were put under the command of the Count of the Saxon Shore and were garrisoned by troops of infantry or cavalry or of both. The *Classis Britannica* seems to have been reorganized into coastal patrols, and part of it became the *Classis Sambrica*, stationed on the Somme to defend the Gallic Saxon Shore.

The peace of the Church, announced by Constantine's edict in 323, the year after the defeat of Maxentius, had its full effect on Britain, as is shown by the attendance of three bishops, a presbyter, and a deacon at the Council of Arles in 314. The bishops were Eborius of York, Restitutus of London and Adelphius of Colonia Londinensium (perhaps Lincoln). The little Christian church at Silchester may date from about this time, perhaps before Constantine's edict.

The high-water mark of peace and prosperity in Roman Britain was reached in the age of Constantine. There were never more houses, towns and villages inhabited. The coins of Constantine are more numerous than those of any other emperor. The working folk in towns and about country houses were perhaps better educated, at least as regards reading and writing, than at any other time onwards down to the 19th century. Coin evidence suggests that about 330 the mile-castles on the Wall were no longer held, the abandonment possibly being due to the fact that pressure was less on this line of defence: the Wall forts were certainly garrisoned for half a century and more later, until the fall of the province was beginning.

M*f* The Death of Constantine to Maximus : 337–383.

After the death of Constantine in 337, the prosperity of the province seems to have continued, but six years later there was an incursion of the Picts, who then probably burnt Corbridge. Constans, then Caesar, came over 342–343 and quieted the immigrant Picts and Scots of the western coasts by making concessions. In 350, after the murder of Constans, Magnentius, the first Briton to rule the whole of the Western Empire, usurped it first in Britain and then in Gaul, but of the consequences of this in Britain nothing is known. Picts and Scots were now devastating the country near the frontier. The usurper overthrown, Julian, appointed Caesar for Gaul by his cousin Constantius II (sole Emperor 350–361), was at Paris, and, being threatened by German invasions, could not leave Gaul, but sent Lupicinus, his *magister militum*, with some lightly-armed Germanic auxiliaries. Crossing from Boulogne to Richborough, they went thence to London, which Lupicinus, like Constantius in 296, made his headquarters. It was now dignified by the title of Augusta, seat of a Procurator, the chief financial officer of the province. Again we are in the dark as to the result of the expedition; but four years later Picts and Saxons, Scots and Attacotti (probably certain groups of Irish) were bringing continuous calamities on the Britons from north, west and south-east.

In 368 came a great disaster: Picts and Scots, Attacotti and others " swamped all the defences of the north and west and poured like a flood over the civilized and prosperous districts ". Nectaridus, the Count, was slain, and Fullofaudes, a Frankish officer, the Dux, was overthrown. The news was brought to the Emperor Valentinian (364–375) in Gaul, who, after some delay, sent Theodosius, father of Theodosius the Great (who may have been in the expedition), to the rescue of Britain. Via Boulogne and Richborough Theodosius went to London, again to serve as H.Q. His first task was to attack and disperse the marauding bands of the enemy near London, and take from them the captives and cattle and booty with which they were laden. Restoring the captives, etc., he kept a small part of the booty for his soldiers; and stayed in London for a time, establishing order and preparing for his northern campaign. Next year (369) he put to flight the marauding tribes, repaired cities and forts, garrisoned and restored the Wall; and then counter-attacked the invaders and ravaged their territory. Welsh districts lately in the hands of the Scotti were incorporated in a new province, to which was granted the title of Valentia (Collingwood).

It is probable that the small stone forts with signal towers that have been excavated on headlands of the Yorkshire coast at Huntcliff, Goldsborough, Ravenscar, Scarborough and Filey, were built as the result of Theodosius' re-fortification of the North. Their position is evidence that the Saxon and possibly Scandinavian raids had spread by the mid 4th century far to the north of the Saxon Shore. Some of them were probably rebuilt before they ended in disaster somewhere about 395 (see Chap. VI).

But in spite of the work of Theodosius and the military settlement in Britain of captive Alemanni, Roman Britain never really recovered from the devastation made by the barbarians after the middle of the 4th century. Country-houses, a good index of prosperity, were numerous to *c.* 350, but coins found in them suggest that some were destroyed or abandoned *c.* 350–360 (*e.g.*, Wiggonholt, Pulborough, Sussex), others a few years later, *c.* 367–368, others were occupied fifteen to twenty years later, and a few, *e.g.*, Ridgewell, Essex, lasted down to the reigns of Arcadius (383–408) and Honorius (395–423). The remains of some of the houses (*e.g.*, Wiggonholt) give evidence of destruction by fire, and the skeletons in them of the massacre of the inhabitants; other ruins point to abandonment and decay; except for wandering bands who during the few years before they were naturally covered with earth lit fires on the mosaic pavements, made fire-places with a few loose tiles, and scattered bones from their meals around the fire (*e.g.*, at Wymondley and Folkestone), they were never again inhabited, not even by the Anglo-Saxons. In the last quarter of a century the country districts were no longer safe, and the dwellers in country-houses who escaped destruction doubtless migrated into the towns, where Roman-Britons held out for varying times behind the walls.

N. *Maximus to Constantine III :* 383–407.

Magnus Clemens Maximus, a Spaniard who held command in Britain and had married a British wife, seized the supreme power in Britain, and in order to obtain the entire Empire, took with him the British troops and crossed to Gaul in 383. He is said to have defeated the Picts and Scots before leaving Britain. On his arrival in Gaul the troops there joined him, and at Paris he defeated Gratian (367–383), who was murdered by one of his own soldiers at Lyons. From his H.Q. at Trier (Treveri), Maximus ruled over Britain, Gaul and Spain, and was recognized as Augustus by the Emperor Theodosius (379–395) until the latter defeated him and put him to death at Aquileia, near Venice, in 388. The troops taken from Britain to Gaul in 383 may have included the whole garrison of Hadrian's Wall and any soldiers there were in Wales. No doubt Maximus intended to restore to Britain the troops he had taken, or he cannot have meant to abandon that part of his empire to be ut to pieces by the barbarians; but he was never able to re-fortify Britain, and the result was disastrous. Picts and Scots were gain on the invasion path, and it cannot have been until after the death of Maximus that Theodosius was able to turn his attention o Britain. But the Wall frontier had now come to an end: there was no more rebuilding. The bringing of relief he assigned to his general Stilicho. Whether Stilicho himself was ever in Britain or not, he reorganized the British army some time about 395: the Dux with his troops to defend the North—*i.e.*, principally the ale of York, but not the Wall—and the Comes the south-east oast. The poet Claudian does not speak of any actual fighting done by Stilicho, but merely says that he fortified (*munivit*) Britain against Scot, Pict and Saxon (395–399). About Stilicho's work here is no certainty. In 401, Arcadius being emperor of the East, and Honorius of the West, Alaric, king of the Visigoths, ntered Italy, and a legion—*i.e.*, an uncertain body of troops, ossibly a detachment of the VIth from York—was called from Britain to help in opposing him.

From the usurpation of Maximus onwards, in spite of the efforts f Stilicho, the condition of Britain went from bad to worse, specially in the north and west: it was enough, and more, to keep he Saxons at bay. In a raid of 405 St. Patrick was taken captive rom his home at Bannaventa (probably near the Bristol Channel) o Ireland. Was this the raid in which King Niall was slain by the ctian Sea (Sea of Wight)?

). *Constantine III and the Evacuation:* 407–410.

In 407 Constantine III followed the precedent of Maximus, and et the seal on the destruction of Britain. A soldier chosen as mperor by the army of Britain, like Maximus, he drained the ountry of its soldiers in order to make a bid for empire on the Continent. In the preceding year (406) two others, Marcus and Gratian, had been chosen, both to be murdered within a few months. Constantine crossed into Gaul with a large part of the army, which ever returned. His departure from the island marks the end of Roman power in Britain. Some soldiers were left here, among them certain Carausius, whose name is on a coin of Constantine III ound at Richborough, of the date 409. Another of his officers, ustinianus, may have built or restored the signal-station of Ravens-ar on the Yorkshire coast: if he is the same as the Justinianus on the nscription, he must have done the work at Ravenscar before 407,

when he went to Gaul with Constantine. Like Maximus a quarter
of a century earlier, Constantine was successful for a while: defeat
ing the barbarians in Gaul, he became master of Gaul and Spain
so that Honorius, unable at the time to defeat him, was obliged to
acknowledge him as an associate in the Empire, as Theodosius had
recognized Maximus. One of his generals, Gerontius, a Briton
thinking himself slighted by Constantine and his son, tried to
overthrow both, and invited the Germans to invade Gaul and
Britain, which they did in 409. Constantine was besieged and killed
by the army of Honorius at Arles in 411, and soon after Gerontius
hard pressed by a conspiracy of his own men, killed himself.

Meanwhile the Roman-Britons, attacked in 409, sent appeals for
help to Honorius, disappointed as they were by the failure of th
Emperor of their own choice, who had left them almost defenceless
Honorius, unable to send any troops (Alaric took Rome in 410)
sent letters to the British cities (*civitates*) bidding them to defend
themselves. They threw off all allegiance to Constantine and sen
out of the country, probably with Honorius' consent, all official
of Constantine's appointment who still remained (410). Colling
wood makes two points clear. First, after 410 Britain was not in
communication with the central government. The coin-series in
Britain goes down to Arcadius and Honorius, and then stops sud
denly. The coins of these emperors, running into thousands
are found at many sites. There is the merest trickle of Constantine
III (*e.g.*, one at Chichester). In Gaul, however, are found coins
down to 474-475. Second, neither Rome nor Britain regarded
the province, which still figures in official documents—*e.g.*, *Notitia*
of 428—as finally severed from the Empire: the Britons appealed
to Rome more than once or twice for aid against their enemies
The finality of separation was not recognized until Britain knew
that further appeals were in vain, and Rome that she could no
longer send help. Till then a restoration of Roman rule was probably
contemplated, and it has been argued that, in spite of the contrary
statement of Procopius, there was a 5th-century reoccupation *c.* 417-
c. 425, probably of the south-east region under a Count of Britain
(Collingwood, *Roman Britain*, pp. 292-301). In any case hope was
definitely dead after a vain appeal (recorded by Gildas) to Aetius in his
third consulate (446). The country districts of Britain were wasted
the towns had fallen one by one, and the rule was passing to the
Angles and Saxons about the middle of the 5th century, though
a settled Saxon government is traditionally dated in the 6th century
Resistance weakened, and the Roman civilization was destroyed
until only vague traditions of it survived in the West, where Angles
and Saxons had not penetrated.

. The End of Roman Britain : 410–c. 450.

The "Romanity" of Britain did not end with the civil and military severance of the province from Rome in 410. In the southern and eastern parts the culture remained Roman until it was destroyed by the Jutes, Saxons and Angles, who wrested the and bit by bit from its inhabitants, driving them from their towns and villages and making their own settlements in hamlets and later a towns, the greater number of which exist to this day. In Wales and Cornwall, which, perhaps with Cumberland, had never been so much Romanized as the East, a Celtic revival began with a certain Roman element in it, and its effects have lasted from the 5th and 6th centuries until now, so that Welsh, not Latin, is spoken in Wales, and the Cornish dialect of Celtic did not die out until about a century and a half ago.

There are not enough materials for even the outlines of a history of the end of Roman Britain. The writers who deal with the strife between the Romanized Britons and the Germanic invaders, and with the settlement of the latter in England, are few, and their statements are seldom precise, often vague and sometimes clearly erroneous. For example, Gildas, who wrote his *De Excidio Britanniae* (*The Destruction of Britain*) about 540, little more than 130 years after Constantine III, had so little knowledge of that century and of the years immediately before it, that he thought the Antonine turf and Hadrianic stone walls were built shortly before that period. St. Bede (*d.* 735), writing more than a century and a half later, used Gildas' writings, and although he was by far the better historian, he does not seem to have known more of the obscure period. The *Historia Brittonum* of Nennius, the *Anglo-Saxon Chronicle* and the Celtic Annals which follow, and add to Gildas, are all now classed as in great measure legendary. At the same time Gildas preserved in his Welsh traditions some facts which may be accepted.

The sketch here attempted is probably accurate in outline: it is drawn from trustworthy writers such as Rhys, McClure and Haverfield. Procopius (6th century) says that after Constantine III Britain was not recovered by the Romans, but continued to be ruled by usurpers (Grk. *tyrannoi*), and we know that Honorius had bidden the cities to defend themselves; the *tyrannoi*, then, were not leaders against the Romans, but native rulers who undertook the defence of the country against the barbarians. Who were they? Possibly the successors of the Dux and of the Comes, the two generals who for more than a century had commanded the garrison troops of the Romans in Britain. Sir John Rhys points out that with the exception of Arthur (called king), the early leaders of the Briton are called in early Welsh literature and tradition *Gwledig* (ruler commander), and not emperor or king; and also that these leaders are said to be of Roman descent, or described as bearing Roman insignia of office.

Two of these rulers at least are probably historical, Ambrosius Aurelianus (or Aurelius Ambrosius), whose deeds are recorded by Gildas and Nennius and in tradition, and Cunedda. Ambrosius was of Roman descent, his relatives had been killed in fighting the Saxons, and as successor of the Count he led the Britons in the south, probably mainly in Wilts, in successful warfare against the Saxons tradition derives the name Amesbury (Ambres-burg) from Ambrosius The campaigns of Ambrosius are placed in the early years of the 5th century, but his descendants or successors were still in power when Gildas wrote some 140 years later. Cunedda is supposed to have been the successor of the Duke: his sphere of command was in the north. His name is Celtic, but his father Edern, his grandfather Padarn and his great-grandfather Tegid bear the Welsh forms of the Latin names Aeternus, Paternus and Tacitus respectively The following details are not claimed as historical, but as embodying a general belief based on historical facts. Cunedda held his court at Carlisle, had 900 horsemen on the Wall, and wore the golden belt, badge of office of a Dux in the later Empire. From the north Cunedda and his sons came into Wales about the time when the Roman armies left Britain. He expelled the Scotti (Irish), probably pirates settled in Wales, and established a supremacy over most of the country, apportioning districts to his sons or nephews, whose names are said to survive where they ruled, *e.g.*, Cardigan (Keredigion) from Keredig, and Merioneth (Meirion) from Meirion Cunedda's dynasty ruled in Wales for many years, and one of his descendants, Maelgwn (Maglocunus), was a warrior of authority and power in the time of Gildas.

Another ruler, of Welsh tradition, is Arthur (perhaps the Latin Artorius), said to have been an early leader—called king—of the Britons against Picts and Saxons and victor in many battles. His existence, not mentioned by Gildas, may be fabulous; but the Arthur legends are known "wherever Celts have spoke a Brythonic language" —*i.e.*, in Scotland, Wales, Cornwall and Brittany; and place-names such as " Arthur's seat " derived from his memory or legend are many wherever the legends are found.

The visit of St. Germanus to Britain in 429 belongs to the period when Picts and Saxons were raiding Britain, but before the Anglo-Saxon settlements had begun, or had spread far west. Saint

Germanus, bishop of Antisiodorum (Auxerre), accompanied by Lupus, bishop of the Tricasini (Troyes), was sent here by Pope St. Celestine to combat the Pelagian heresy. (This was directed against the doctrine of Grace as taught by Augustine, namely that the power of man to do great things does not originate in man's will, but in God. Pelagius thought that this doctrine denied human freedom and weakened the will to self-discipline.) He seems to have gone northwards and north-westwards and to have confuted the heretical teachers somewhere beyond Verulam, the Roman town which was replaced by St. Albans. Here he stayed on his return, to give thanks to God at the tomb of St. Alban. Leaving Verulam, he was delayed by an accident, but after recovery he was journeying when he received news of a Saxon and Pictish war. In his earlier years he had been a soldier, and with Lupus he headed the British host, many of whom were newly baptized, the season being Easter. The enemy was met in a valley, and the Britons, instructed by St. Germanus, raised the cry " Alleluia ". The hills re-echoed the sound, and the enemy fled without striking a blow, many of them being drowned in crossing a river.

Some eighteen years later St. Germanus was again in Britain, accompanied by Severus, bishop of the Treveri (Trier), and, as Bede says, they found the people constant in the faith as they had been left.

The Anglo-Saxon settlements constitute the second and final stage of the destruction of Roman Britain, but that period falls outside the scope of the present volume. It is generally true that the fate of most Romanized Britons was slaughter or slavery or flight to Wales or beyond the sea to Brittany, or existence in isolated places such as mountains and forests: the dense woodlands even of the Weald of Sussex and Surrey appear to have harboured some. The modern upshot of the four centuries of Roman occupation is that the Englishman, while he has some Celtic blood in his veins, has inherited very little, if any, Roman-British civilization, which in his state of barbarism he utterly destroyed.

Q. *The Celtic Revival.*

It is probable that from the time of the isolation of Britain from the Empire there existed a " Latinizing " party and a party adverse to it. The strongest Roman or rather Roman–British element would be the inhabitants of the larger towns, London, Colchester, York and the rest, and as these were cut off or dispossessed, the Celtic party would increase in strength. In the time of Gildas, princes like Constantine of Dumnonia, Aurelius Caninus and others were thirsting for civil war: Celtic rivalry and jealousy were rife then as in the days of Julius Caesar and Agricola and in the later days of Welsh strife with Norman and English. Had the Celts of this country been able to act continuously and consistently in combination under their rulers, they would have been far more difficult to conquer by Romans or English. As it was, they combined only when great danger or distress came on them, in the campaigns of Caesar or Agricola, and also when the Angles and Saxons were worse enemies than the Romans had ever been. These enemies were the main cause of the Celtic Revival of the 5th and 6th centuries, and that revival was Celtic rather than Roman-Celtic because it could be brought about only in the more secure West, where the people were more Celtic than Roman, and not in the more Roman East, which was being destroyed piecemeal. Other causes of the Celtic Revival were Irish immigration and settlements, in both north and south. In the beginning of the 5th century the Irish settlements in Caledonia were growing quickly, and a colony of Irish Celts had also perhaps reached Silchester in time to set up an Ogam stone to one Ebicatos before the town was abandoned, probably in the 5th century.

But the Saxon settlement of the lowland zone, cut off from the Empire and all its influences, was the main cause. Some of the Romanized Celts of the east fled from their enemies to the west, and, leaving the Roman towns and villages behind, went into a district where Celtic influence was strong. Others migrated from the east to Brittany, but a still greater number, to judge by their names, migrated from Devon and Cornwall. The numbers of the immigrants into Gaul were great; and the immigration went on from the 5th into the 7th century. The Celts, then, who were left in Britain with powerful enemies pressing on them, were forced into a " unitary national conscience " like the Fascists of modern Italy: witness the name by which they called themselves, Kymry (Combroges), meaning fellow-countrymen. This unity began in the early part of the 5th century, when tradition says that Cunedda, who ruled at first in the north, came into Wales, and seems to have been the first to establish a sort of kingdom which stretched from far north of Cumberland to South Wales, and which endured for 200 years.

How far the Western Celts, among whom the Celtic Revival arose, were Romanized is uncertain, but some degree of Romanization is certain, and there is evidence that it survived. The post-Roman inscriptions from Wales and Dumnonia, of the 6th and possibly of the 5th and 7th centuries, are mostly in Latin, "which seems to have continued to be the official and learned tongue", but in some two dozen cases the Latin is accompanied by a Goidelic version in the Ogam script, an adaptation of the Latin by a Goidel and invented probably in Ireland. Besides the Latin names of Gildas' contemporaries—*e.g.*, Constantinus, Aurelius Caninus (Conan)—others are found in the Welsh genealogies in Welsh forms—*e.g.*, Aergol (Agricola), Dunod (Donatus), Meurig (Mauricius). And Latin culture-words are found in Welsh, some as survivals, some as later introductions—*e.g.*, ystaffel (stabulum) = room, pared (pariet-em) = partition, ffenestr' (fenestra) = window: these are quoted by Wheeler as "borrowed, doubtless with the idea themselves", by the Celts from the Romans. If so, these borrowings would have been made long before the 6th century. In the sub-Roman period, says Collingwood, "men lived on the relics of Romanity diluted in a pervading medium of Celticism".

CHAPTER II

LEGIONS, CAMPS, FORTS, FLEET, THE WALLS

THE Roman army of the early Empire in Britain, as elsewhere, consisted of: (i) the Legions, composed of Roman citizens, first-class troops, and (ii) the Auxilia, regiments of infantry or cavalry, composed of non-citizens, and recruited from the provinces, though not from " burgess towns "—i.e., privileged towns with the status of *municipia* or *coloniae*. Both Legions and Auxiliaries had in the 2nd century become almost entirely frontier defenders, the House-hold Troops (Praetorian Guards and Equites Singulares) at Rome being the sole exceptions. This system, however, proved inadequate to withstand the strain of barbarian onslaughts at the frontiers in the 3rd century, and when Diocletian and Constantine had breathing spaces secured by victory over barbarians and usurpers, they re-organized both the civil and military administration of the Empire. Many of the older Legions and Auxiliary Cohorts and Alae still appear, but they are grouped in the two main divisions of the army: (a) the Palatini and Comitenses, who followed the Emperor and the *magistri peditum* and *equitum*; these were the field army which went to war at need; (b) the Limitanei or Ripenses, under the *duces limitum*, formed the territorial frontier guard, stationed in forts at the boundaries of the provinces.

Much of our information on military matters is derived from the *Notitia Dignitatum*, an Official List of the Civil and Military Officers, with bodies of troops and their stations, of the Empire in the time of Arcadius and Honorius; its date, as we have it, is put at A.D. 428—i.e., in the reign of Valentinian III. It is, of course, out of date as regards Britain, which was severed from the Empire in 407-410 (Chap. I, Section O). The portion dealing with Britain is puzzling: in the section *per lineam valli* (along the line of the wall) it is clearly defective, and the arrangement suggests that the list of troops is a survival of a much older list. Still, regiments, *e.g.*, *ala Herculea*, are named that cannot have had their titles before the end of the 3rd or beginning of the 4th century. In the *Notitia* a Count of Britain is mentioned as at the head of a field army, but he is not mentioned in Ammianus' account of the disaster of 368 (I–M), and it seems possible that the Count was not created till after the evacuation, and then for the purpose of the reconquest of Britain, which was never carried out (Collingwood). He would have been one of the commanders of the Comitenses, and would have ranked above the *duces limitum*. The Legions were much

44

altered: *vexillationes* (detachments) of legions are found separated for special service in different places; and in the middle of the 4th century a legion, originally of 5000 to 6000 infantry, could not have numbered more than 1500.

In Britain from the time of Hadrian there were three Legions— II, VI and XX. From about 70 the IInd was at Caerleon in south Wales. It was apparently moved in the 4th century to Richborough, then the H.Q. of the Count of the Saxon Shore; but it could not have been more than 1000 men strong, as Richborough fort comprised less than 5 acres. Caerleon was 51 acres. What became of the rest of this legion? Did a part remain at Caerleon? The VIth was at York, H.Q. of the Dux Britanniarum till late times: it is found there in the *Notitia*, but in what strength is not known. The XXth was at Chester from 48 onwards, certainly till towards the end of the 3rd century, and, though not mentioned in the *Notitia*, it may have been counted as part of the army of the Count of Britain.

These three legions and the highland country around them stand for the military area of Britain: Caerleon for the west, Chester for the north-west, and York for the north. All the rest of the country—the midland, south-east, south and south-west— formed the lowland civil zone, where Romanization was strongest. In the peaceful lowlands were no troops. At Caerleon you may still see remains of the Roman walls, but at York and Chester cathedral cities have grown up on the sites, though here, as so often, medieval partly mark the Roman walls. The Multangular Tower at York is a remnant of late Roman defences. But the first line of defence was the auxiliaries in their forts on the frontiers. We know of a round hundred of such forts (*castella*), not all co-existent: some twenty or more in Wales, sixty or seventy in North England, inclusive of those on Hadrian's Wall, and about thirty-four north of it, including those of the Antonine Wall. The *Notitia* mentions thirty-eight in north Britain in the late 3rd century.

The forts (*castra stativa*) occupied by the legions were of 50–60 acres, those occupied by the auxiliaries (*castella*) averaged *c.* 5 acres, and were distributed according to military need along frontiers, roads or in awkward country. Both types were laid out on one model, with a general resemblance to the scheme of a camp. A square or oblong enclosure with rounded corners was protected with rampart and V-shaped ditch or ditches separated from the outer face of the wall by a berm, and had four gates placed symmetrically (not necessarily at the centre of the sides). In the middle where the streets met was the H.Q. and shrine for the worship of the soldiers. Near by were the commander's house and officers' quarters and the store-houses, including granaries; at the ends were barracks, stables and so on. The ramparts were in the 1st century made of earth, clay and sod, sometimes with a facing of stones, but later stone ramparts backed by an earthen bank were general. The largest H.Q. building (*principia*) found in Britain was at Newstead, a stone building of 131 by 104 ft. The floors of granaries were raised some $2\frac{1}{2}$ ft. above the general surface-level and supported by sleeper walls or low stone pillars, the basement being ventilated by small openings. Barracks were long and narrow, divided by cross walls into many rooms. Bath-houses were detached buildings outside the gates, with hypocausts (underground hot chambers), hot room, cold-water bath, dressing-rooms and so on. A bath-house was a place of recreation, a club-house where the men had a flutter at games of chance, and made offerings at the altar of Fortune for luck.

Outside the ramparts were settlements of camp-followers (*canabae*).

The Walls are good examples of the Roman artificial frontier, sometimes a road with ditch in front and forts along it, sometimes ditch, mound and wall, and forts. The fortification of the Hadrianic *limes* was not uniform from end to end, but was carried on in stages, one following another as it was found necessary. Bede was the first to give a clear description of Wall and *Vallum*. First the *vallum* (*limes*), seen south of the Wall at varying distances, and consisting of a flat-bottomed ditch, 30 ft. wide and 7 ft. deep, the upcast of which has been made into mounds, one on each side of the ditch, each *c.* 6 ft. high and 20 ft. across, and separated from the ditch by a berm of 24 ft. wide. The whole system is 100–150 ft. across. Gaps were made in it at intervals of *c.* 45 yds. while stone was being quarried and brought to the Wall. The *vallum* is $7\frac{1}{2}$ miles shorter than the wall. Second, the Wall of concrete faced with stone, to a general thickness of 10 ft. in places and $7\frac{1}{2}$ ft. in others, and original height of *c.* 16–18 ft., exclusive of the parapet: it had a walk along the top 4–5 ft. broad. Here again there was no strict uniformity. It is now clear from recent investigations that there first existed the *vallum* with small isolated forts to its north; that next the forts were enlarged; then the wall was built to connect isolated forts. A broad 10-ft. wall with 11-ft. foundations was planned from Newcastle to Stanwix near Carlisle. From both these points a narrower $7\frac{1}{2}$-ft. wall was made—*i.e.*, to Wallsend, where a new fort was erected, and to Burgh Marsh on Solway. The full broad Wall had been made from Newcastle to Heddon when the order was given to reduce the breadth. An exception to the broad wall was in the sector of the Irthing Gorge, where a turf wall was substituted, but this was superseded by the narrow wall. A western sector, Burgh Marsh to Bowness, 9 ft. thick, was probably added in the Antonine period (C. F. C. Hawkes). Bonded into and part of the Wall were milecastles and turrets. The former were small forts 70 ft. × 60 ft. to 60 ft. × 50 ft., attached to the south side of the Wall. They occur at fairly regular intervals of a Roman mile, and their internal buildings could house c. 100 men. Two signalling turrets occur between the milecastles, thus dividing the mile into three; they were c. 13 ft. square internally, and contained a staircase to the top of the Wall. They served as signal stations and shelters for sentry groups; and similar turrets were erected along the Cumberland coast—e.g., at Beckfoot, Maryport and Moresby. The Wall is 73 miles long. Third, the Military Way, running near (south of) the Wall, and joining up the forts, with branches to the milecastles and paths to the turrets. Fourth, the Ditch, in front (north) of the Wall, separated from it by a berm of c. 22 ft. and V-shaped, normally 35 ft. wide and 10 ft. deep. It is dispensed with where the Wall is on the edge of precipitous rock. And fifth, the seventeen Forts at intervals varying from 2 to 8 miles, 5 miles being a normal distance. They are in two sizes, the smaller of c. 2½ acres, to hold a cohort of 500 men, the larger of 4–5 acres for a cohort of 1000 men, according to the principle that permanent forts accommodated 200–250 men per acre. The sites often had regard to a southern aspect, and always to water supply.

Here is a list of the Forts from east to west:—

1. Wallsend (Segedunum). 2. Newcastle (Pons Aelii). 3. Benwell (Condercum). 4. Rudchester (Vindobala). 5. Halton (Hunnum). 6. Chesters (Cilurnum). 7. Carrawburgh (Procolitia). 8. Housesteads (Borcovicium). 9. Chesterholm (Vindolanda). 10. Great Chesters (Aesica). 11. Carvoran (Magnae). 12. Birdoswald (Camboglanna). 13. Castlesteads. 14. Stanwix. 15. Burgh-by-Sands. 16. Drumburgh. 17. Bowness on Solway.

All are actually on the line of the Wall save Chesterholm and Carvoran, which are on the Stanegate, south of the Wall and vallum—older forts made by Agricola or later, and afterwards included in Hadrian's system. Castlesteads is south of the Wall, but north of the vallum, not on the Stanegate. Probably the wall-builders chose a more convenient course across the Cambeck valley. Perhaps the best-preserved stretch of the Wall is near No. 8, Borcovicium, slightly west of where the Watling Street crosses the Wall from Corbridge.

Excavations, revealing in forts and milecastles three floors with datable coins and debris on them, have established the following facts. The *vallum*, the Forts and the Wall are Hadrianic, the first occupation ending in a disaster about A.D. 180. There was a rebuilding and a second occupation, also ending in a disaster soon after 270. The third occupation after rebuilding or restoration lasted in the milecastle till *c.* 330. Coincidence shows that the Wall Forts were occupied till *c.* 383. Visible and tangible objects connected with the Wall are best seen at Chesters (Cilurnum) on the North Tyne, where there is a museum established by Mr. John Clayton.

For the Antonine Wall see I–H. We may add the names of the forts from Forth to Clyde.

1. Bridgeness. 2. Kinneil.. 3. Inveravon. 4. Mumrills. 5. Falkirk. 6. Rough Castle. 7. Seabeg. 8. Castlecary. 9. Westerwood. 10. Croy Hill. 11. Bar Hill. 12. Auchendavy. 13. Kirkintilloch. 14. Cadder. 15. Balmuildy. 16. New Kilpatrick. 17. Castle Hill. 18. Duntocher. 19. Old Kilpatrick.

For most of the distance rampart and ditch are still visible, undulating across the isthmus with a course strategically as direct as possible, and taking advantage of high ground so as to command valley or low-lying ground in front. Nos. 9, 10 and 11 are at a considerable elevation on the watershed of the isthmus.

A third frontier defence was the *Classis Britannica* (British Fleet), a standing fleet dating probably from the time of Claudius. From the beginning till *c.* 300 it was organized at, and administered from, Gessoriacum (Boulogne) as H.Q., the chief stations in Britain being Dover and Lympne, and from time to time Newcastle, *ad vallum Hadriani*. Agricola paid special attention to his naval arm, in 78 personally supervising the sounding of the Scottish estuaries, and in 83 securing concerted action between legions and fleet. An inscription records L. Tusidius Campester as Prefect of the British Fleet and Procurator of Britain. The busiest time of the fleet was 258–296. first in connection with the five Gaulish emperors recognized in Britain, Postumus to Tetricus. The history of Carausius and Constantius has been traced in Ch. I, K and L. After 300, according to the generally accepted view, the British Fleet was disbanded: there is no mention of it in *Notitia* or Ammianus. Some sort of reorganisation and division must have taken place— *e.g.*, some ships were made over to each harbour and put at the disposal of the fort commandant.

The men of the fleet (*classiarii*) probably spent more time ashore than afloat. Triremes had to choose fair weather for their voyages, making not more than 4 miles an hour, and so taking seven or eight hours to cross from Dover to Boulogne. Their business was to patrol the seas separating south-east England from the mouths of the Rhine and part of the coast of Gaul, and so to protect the line of communication and Channel commerce; to keep down piracy and smuggling (there were *portoria*, harbour dues, to pay), to help provision soldiers stationed in harbours and coastal forts and the troops on the Wall; and to supply transports whenever military expeditions were made on either coast—*e.g.*, when Hadrian arrived in the Tyne to plan the Wall, and when Severus landed a force for his invasion of Caledonia. Unfortified Roman villas on the south-east coast—*e.g.*, at Mersea, Folkestone and Eastbourne—seem to show that piracy was not a great danger, at any rate in the earlier empire. Handymen, the *classiarii* made bricks and tiles, built their own quarters, quarried stone and chalk, repaired their quays, built transports, etc. The fleet consisted of warships (*naves longae*) and transports (*naves onerariae*). The triremes, called *liburnae*, rowed three banks of oars, some sixty in all, and were further aided by sails. The *remiges* rowed, the *nautae* trimmed the sails, while the fighting was done by the marines (*propugnatores*). The fleet was commanded by a *praefectus*, with perhaps 200 triremes normally in his command, and H.Q. at Gessoriacum. A division of the fleet was under a *praepositus*, and quartered at one of the principal harbours. A captain of a trireme (*trierarch*) commanded *c.* 200 men, enlisted among the allies, freedmen or slaves, generally not natives of Britain, but of Gaul, Spain, the Danube countries, or the Eastern or Central Mediterranean. They had Latin status while serving, and Roman citizenship on discharge after twenty-six years. Their status was much inferior to that of the legionaries.

Constantius I took in hand the task of organizing the *Forts of the Saxon Shore*, probably between 296 and 306. Our knowledge of them is derived from the *Notitia* and archaeological research. In the *Notitia* are given the insignia of the Count of the Saxon Shore, the places under his control, the forces occupying these places, and the staff of officials allotted to him. The forts are given in geographical order in Ch. I, L. The strategic purpose of each is clear. Brancaster, in Norfolk, protected the entrance of the Wash; Burgh Castle, Suffolk, the river Yare; Bradwell-on-Sea, Essex, the south Essex flats; Reculver, Kent, the mouth of the Thames and the channel round Thanet to Richborough; Richborough, Kent, this channel and the beginning of Watling Street; Dover, the roads to Canterbury and west Kent; Lympne, the lowlands and tidal estuaries of south Kent; Pevensey, Sussex, the flats of south-east Sussex and the Weald; and Portchester, Hants, the road to Winchester and the Silchester region. Possibly Walton Castle, which was near Felixstowe, and is now under the sea, not Bradwell, was Othona:

it guarded the rivers Deben, Orwell, Stour, and Colne and the district north of Colchester. All these forts had thick walls and external bastions of the same character, and have yielded remains suggestive of the 4th century. This not really efficient coastguard system was established over a seaboard extending for more than 380 miles: 200 from the Wash to Tilbury, and 180 from Gravesend to Portsmouth. It seems to have served its purpose till *c.* 350.

Archaeology points to Richborough, Dover, Lympne, Pevensey and Portchester as the five forts newly constructed about 300, of which Dover, Lympne and Pevensey had been active as harbours of the British Fleet from the 1st century. Richborough was a harbour and a permanent camp from soon after 43. Dover had its octagonal pharos or light tower on Castle Hill, and a similar one on the western heights from Claudian times: its fort was situated where now is the Market Place. Its importance as a signalling centre was great, and owing to the nature of the tides it was the natural landing-place after a crossing from Boulogne. The defence of the opposite Gaulish coast, also called the Saxon Shore, was carried out by a *Classis Sambrica*, so called from the river Samara, now the Somme.

In the latter half of the 4th century a system of small signalling forts was established along the north-east coast, from north Yorkshire to the Wash, but these were built on high cliffs, and not connected with harbours. Huntcliff, near Saltburn, Goldsborough, Ravenscar, Scarborough and Filey have been proved by excavation, and there were probably more. They may have been built as the result of Theodosius' re-fortification of the north (Ch. I, N): Saxon and Scandinavian raids had spread far north of the Saxon Shore.

Such being the general system of defence, we may describe in outline a few special forts. York (Eburacum), a British town, was occupied early by Cerialis (71–74), and the IXth Hispana legion was established there, to be succeeded by the VIth Augusta. The first fort had a clay rampart and timber barracks, a typical Flavian fort. The legionary fortress was on the east bank of the Ouse, with dimensions of 550 yds. south-west to north-east, 468 yds. north-west to south-east, and an area of *c.* 53 acres—*i.e.*, larger than Caerleon (Isca Silurum) but smaller than Chester (Deva). On the west bank was the *colonia*, also fortified, probably dating from the end of the 2nd or beginning of the 3rd century. Eburacum was the military capital and had a *palatium*; it was the base of Agricola's second northern expedition, and of many later ones. Severus and Constantius Chlorus died there. (See *Roman York*, Gordon Home.)

Templeborough, near Rotherham (possibly the Morbium of the *Notitia*), another Flavian clay-rampart fort like York and Ilkley, guarded the eastern length of the road crossing the highlands (Pennine Hills) of Derbyshire and Yorkshire, between the lowlands of Cheshire and south Lancashire and those of south Yorkshire. Other forts serving this purpose were the Derbyshire Melandra Castle and Brough (Anavio), both giving evidence of early and late occupation. The remains of Templeborough fort were destroyed by the erection of a steel factory during 1916, but for eight months during the destruction Mr. Thos. May directed possible excavations. The fort was probably occupied within a few years of A.D. 50 (thus one of the few Claudian forts known in Britain), and continuously till the reign of Marcus Aurelius, "with a special period of activity . . . in the stormy Trajan–Hadrian period". At this time the *praetorium* was rebuilt in stone, the size of the fort reduced, but the baths enlarged. First an advance-guard, later it was a rear-guard against the Brigantes. In the 3rd century, after a gap of feeble occupation, there was a stronger tenure. The dimensions of the fort being *c.* 200 × 120 yds., it would have accommodated a *cohors milliaria*. About 13 miles south-west of Doncaster (?Danum), Templeborough was perhaps connected with it by Roman road.

The following three forts guarded the main road from York to Carlisle and the Wall over a length of 30 miles. Bowes (Lavatrae), above the river Greta, is *c.* 140 yds. square, in the north corner of which are the ruins of Bowes Castle. Bowes with Brough (Verterae) and Kirkby Thore (Bravoniacum) together guard the road as it passes over the "backbone" between the lower lands of north Yorks and those of Cumberland, Bowes being near the east edge and Brough about midway in the 25 miles on to Kirkby Thore, which is in the Eden valley, where it widens out. Brough measures 157 × 113 yds. Kirkby Thore was at a junction of three roads: (i) York to Carlisle and the west end of the Wall, and the inland and port forts of the Cumberland coast; (ii) the "Maiden Way" over high ground (*c.* 2000 ft.) north from Kirkby Thore, to the Wall at Carvoran (Magnae), near the fort of Birdoswald (Camboglanna)—i.e., to the centre and most critical part of the Wall—and (iii) nearly due south, to Chester via Kendal, Ribchester and Manchester. On the main road from York to Corbridge was Lanchester (Longovicium). It could accommodate in its area of over 6 acres a cohort of 1000 men.

From these northern forts we turn to three samples of the Saxon Shore Forts, at Pevensey, Porchester and Richborough. Pevensey

(Anderida) was a fortified port to the gates of which ships coul
come, and although now nearly a mile inland, it was in Roma

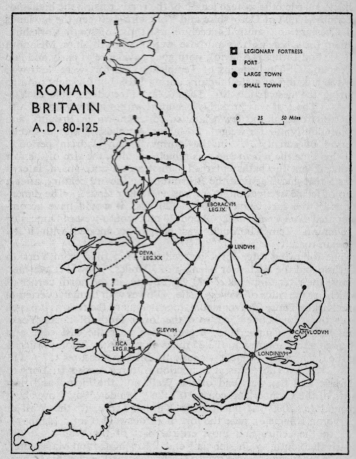

ROMAN
BRITAIN
A.D. 80-125

☐ LEGIONARY FORTRESS
■ FORT
● LARGE TOWN
• SMALL TOWN

0   25   50 Miles

EBORACVM
LEG.IX.

DEVA
LEG.XX

LINDVM

GLEVVM

ISCA
LEG.II

CAMVLODVM

LONDINIVM

FIG. 3.—Roads, Forts and Towns in the great period of Romanization

times on the shore of what was almost, if not quite, an island. Th
coin evidence is from 253 to 383, but a tile stamped with the name o
the Emperor Honorius brings us to the years following 395. Th

garrison of some thousand Abulci was quartered in wooden hutments. The fort differs in shape from the other forts, being roughly ovoid with greatest diameter west–east, so made to suit the ground contours; it measures 986 ft. by *c.* 535 ft., and contains over $8\frac{1}{4}$ acres, the largest of the Saxon Shore forts except Lympne. The wall was 20–30 ft. high and 10 ft. thick, supported by twelve bastions equal in height to the wall: to-day ten towers are standing. Their shape is a semi-circle added to a rectangle, the latter adjoining the wall, to which it was bonded; the rectangular portion has parallel sides of *c.* 10–12 ft. The wall, of flint and rubble cemented, is faced on the outside with hard sandstone and bonding courses (generally two together) of red tiles, on the inside with stone and flints, but the construction is very irregular. The main entrance is on the west side, the gateway consisting of a hollow square *c.* 18 ft. each way inside the line of the curtain wall which approached it obliquely from either side. It had a tower set out on the wall on either side. The barbican was spanned by two arches, one forming the outer entrance, another being a few yards farther in; between them was a guardroom 18 ft. square. There were three other gates—east, north, and a south postern.

Portchester fort is exceptionally regular in shape, roughly a square of about 600 ft., with a water-gate in the middle of the eastern side: its bastions are of the same type as those of Pevensey. As it is to-day, it is the most remarkable monument of its kind in Britain. High tides in Portsmouth harbour still wash the foot of the walls. In the north-west corner, as in the south-east corner at Pevensey, are the remains of a Norman castle, and in the south-west a 12th-century church (Plate IV).

Richborough (Rutupiae) was the chief port of disembarkation, and stood on an island in the estuary of the Stour, but connected with the mainland by a causeway. Part of the fortifications thrown up by the legions of Aulus Plautius on landing can still be seen. The place at once became a military depot with large store-houses, and towards the end of the 1st century was built a huge monument cased with Italian marble—probably to commemorate the conquest of Britain. The triple ditches now to be seen were the defences of a small fort established in the 3rd century against the Saxon pirates; but this shortly afterwards was replaced by a larger fort enclosed by the extant stone walls, 11 ft. thick and still in places 25 ft. high. This was surrounded by a double ditch. Civilian buildings grew up round the fort, and there was an amphitheatre, as at Silchester, Caerleon, Chichester and elsewhere. A museum on the site preserves a selection of the more important finds ".

CHAPTER III

ROADS, ROAD-STATIONS, BRIDGES, MILESTONES, ETC.

THE Romanization of Britain was effected as much by the system of roads as by any other single factor. It is fallacious to suppose that people like the Belgae, possessing a high degree of civilization failed to make and maintain very passable road communication for a whole century before the Roman conquest. Silchester must thus have been connected with Southampton, and St. Albans with Colchester. But Roman military engineers must have often straightened and hardened many lengths of the traditional and Belgic tracks to meet the needs of the armies of conquest. Within a few years after A.D. 43 the great main roads were surveyed and constructed, and very long stretches of many of these remain in use today as first-class roads, while in other cases the course of a Roman road is lost for many miles across the woods, ploughed and pasture-fields, and moors, its functions having been usurped by more modern routes linking Saxon villages and medieval townships.

We may trace the main trunk roads which a traveller of the 3rd century might have traversed after landing at one of the four east Kent ports, Reculver, Richborough, Dover or Lympne. The roads from all of these met after a few miles at Canterbury (Durovernum). Thence westwards it was a straight run to Rochester (Durobrivae) where the Medway was forded, with a slight turn north to Springhead (Vagniacae), and so in a straight run through Dartford by Shooter's Hill to London (Londinium). Apart from the Watling Street along which we have come, there are no less than eight roads branching from London, or a few miles out. London is the most important road centre; but Silchester and Cirencester are both five dials. Beginning on the south, there are three running through Surrey and Sussex: first, one through Titsey and Ashdown Forest to Lewes, a route for the transport of Sussex iron; next, one through Streatham and Godstone to Hassocks, and thence presumably to the well-populated coast near Brighton and Portslade; and a third, the Sussex Stane Street, through Ewell, Dorking, Billingshurst and Pulborough, and over the South Downs to Chichester. But these are comparatively minor matters, and we must set out for the west and south-west, by Brentford, Hounslow and Staines to Silchester, which gives us three choices—south-south-west to Winchester and Southampton, south-west by the Portway to Old Sarum and Dorchester, and north-west to Speen, Cirencester and

Gloucester, and so by the coasts of the Severn and south Wales to Caerleon (Isca Silurum), Neath and Carmarthen. Near Speen the road branches for Marlborough, Bath and Sea Mills near Bristol; and at Old Sarum for the lead mines of Mendip and Weston-super-Mare (Axium). From Dorchester is the road to Exeter (Isca Dumnoniorum). We are taking no account here of numerous cross-roads linking up the routes we have traced. But mention must be made of the Fosse Way starting from Seaton or Exeter and going north-east by way of Ilchester to Bath, Cirencester, Chesterton and Leicester to Lincoln. This was made early as a frontier road (*limes*), roughly delimiting the lowland or civil from the highland or military area. It is, for its length, the most direct road in Britain. Starting from London again by Edgware Road and Kilburn, we follow the main road (Watling Street) to the north-west, through St. Albans, a fashionable town with a theatre, Dunstable, Stony Stratford, Towcester, High Cross (Venonae), across the Fosse Way, through Mancetter and Penkridge, a little south to Wroxeter (Viroconium), where we join the east Wales road coming up from the south at Kenchester, and so proceed to Chester (Deva).

Next is perhaps the longest and most important route of all, from London (Bishopsgate) to the North by the East Coast. The main points are: Braughing (Herts), Godmanchester (Cambs.), Castor (Northants), Lincoln, Brough on the north shore of the Humber, York, Aldborough, Catterick, Binchester, Lanchester, Ebchester, Corbridge on Tyne, crossing Hadrian's Wall near Halton (Hunnum), by Risingham to High Rochester (Bremenium), Cappuck and Newstead (Trimontium). The road from York to Newstead through the counties of Yorks, Durham and Northumberland, 140 miles in all, is most pleasantly described in detail by Miss Jessie Mothersole in her book *Agricola's Road into Scotland*. Hence the way to Inveresk on the Firth of Forth is uncertain; but the route would be by Cramond and westward along the military way of the Antonine Wall to Falkirk and Camelon, and then again north to Ardoch, Strageath, Gask, Grassy Walls and a few miles farther up the river Tay, where the road came to an end. From Chester the main north-west route lay through Manchester, Ribchester, Overborough, Brougham and Carlisle (Luguvallium). At Stanwix Hadrian's Wall was crossed to Netherby, and thence the road ran more to the west by Birrens (Blatobulgium) to Clyde Burn on the watershed between Solway and Clyde. Roads from Carlisle and Brougham led to the Cumberland coast at Maryport (Uxellodunum) and Ravenglass (Clanoventa).

Important cross roads between the main east and west route
were from north of Catterick by Bowes, Brough and Kirkby Thor
to Brougham (see Chap. II); farther south from York, by Tad
caster, Ilkley (Olicana), thence either to Ribchester or Manchester
and still farther south, from Doncaster, via Templeborough and th
Yorkshire Brough (Anavio), to Melandra and Manchester; an
from Braughing to Cirencester westwards by St. Albans an
Alchester.

Finally we have to direct travellers to East Anglia. The mai
road is north-east from London to Chelmsford (Caesaromagus)
Kelvedon, Colchester and Stonham (Suffolk) to Caistor by Norwic
(Venta Icenorum). From Chelmsford a more northerly road ra
round the east of the Fens to the Wash near Brancaster. Colcheste
was connected with St. Albans by a route running directly west t
Braughing, and thence south-west by Welwyn; and with God
manchester on the main north road by Bartlow, crossing th
Icknield Way, and so by Cambridge.

Such were the principal roads (see *Ordnance Survey Map c
Roman Britain* and *Roman Roads in Britain*, by Thos. Codrington
1928). Many more remain to be discovered, or completed b
finding sections linking up stretches already known—*e.g.*, it i
certain that there were Roman roads for the tin traffic in Cornwal
as four milestones have been found there, and there were certainl
other roads in Lincolnshire. The original authority on Roma
roads is the *Antonine Itinerary*, a traveller's road-book compile
by a Roman official. The British section of it contains fiftee
routes, giving distances from place to place along these route
It is obvious that its sources vary in date and that the measure
ments in miles are not scientifically accurate. The compilatio
probably belongs to the years 211–18, when Antoninus, whos
nickname was Caracalla, was emperor.

The rest of this chapter will deal briefly with the constructio
of the roads, road stations, bridges, fords, milestones, etc. As t
construction, two popular fallacies are hard to dispel: that Roma
roads run perfectly straight from start to finish, and that they wer
always made with a surface of laid stone slabs. These I will refut
by describing two roads with which I am intimately acquainte
The Winchester–Silchester road is over 23 miles long. Though it
never much out of the straight, it has eight changes of directio
not counting the uncertain short stretch from the Roman walls c
Winchester to King's Worthy. It is true that there are no grea
obstacles to be overcome, and that a large part of the course
over gently undulating chalk hills. Starting from King's Worth

on a bearing of $27\frac{3}{4}°$ E. of true N., its first limb is $9\frac{1}{2}$ miles long to a little north of Bradley Farm, practically all modern road. Here an angle of $11\frac{3}{4}°$ to the east is turned and the course is $2\frac{7}{8}$ miles to the *Sun* Inn on the Winchester–Basingstoke road. At the inn an angle of $2\frac{1}{2}°$ W. enables the road to run up a shallow valley between two 500-ft. contours, and so to reach its highest point, over 500 ft., in $1\frac{3}{8}$ miles at a point north-west of Kempshott House. The fourth limb of $6\frac{5}{8}$ miles, at an angle of $14\frac{1}{2}°$ more W., completes the journey on the chalk and begins that on the clay at Sherborne St. John to a point west of Beaurepaire Park. The fifth stretch, turning an angle of $4°$ W., brings us in $1\frac{1}{4}$ miles to Latchmore Green, and the sixth, angle $2\frac{1}{2}$ °E., to Three Ashes cross roads in $\frac{3}{4}$ mile: both these turns are matters of minor convenience, the avoidance of small hills of 250 ft. contour. Seventh, from Three Ashes in $\frac{5}{8}$ mile to a point in Church Lane, at an angle of $8°$ W.; and finally the eighth limb makes a bold turn W. of $16\frac{1}{2}°$ in order to go straight into the south gate of Silchester in *c.* 280 yards. The original bearing out of King's Worthy continued for the whole length of the route would have brought the road some $1\frac{1}{4}$ miles east of the south gate. Such were the changes of direction in a comparatively short road over ground which is comparatively easy.

The second road,[1] Stane Street from Chichester to London, through Sussex and Surrey, is also in eight limbs, but owing to the obstacles of the South Downs, the Arun flats at Pulborough and the course of the Mole through Dorking Gap, it diverges much more from a straight line. Its length is *c.* $58\frac{1}{4}$ miles, and in its course it deviates from a direct line, which would have taken it west of Petworth, by a maximum of over 5 miles a little north of Pulborough. The road is constructed on three main alignments, 1. Chichester to Hardham Camp; 2. Todhurst Farm to Anstie Grange on the sandhills south of Dorking, and 3. Nonsuch Park to London Bridge. There are many minor changes of direction within and between these main alignments, in which the road was probably laid independently and ultimately linked up by sections such as that between Dorking and Ewell. There was no difficulty in making the trace of the road by smoke or other signals: convenient heights were the crest of the South Downs at Gumber, Borough Hill (Pulborough), Leith Hill, Brockham Warren by Box Hill, and Epsom Downs. As Codrington points out, " there can be no doubt that the Roman engineers made use of a method well known to surveyors for laying out a straight line between extreme points not visible from each other, from two or more intermediate points

[1] See *With a Spade on Stane Street*, S. E. Winbolt (Methuen).

from which the extreme points are visible. By shifting the intermediate points alternately all are brought to lie in a straight line.''

In laying out Roman roads in Britain, use was made of the *groma* (model in Science Museum, South Kensington), being adapted for sighting long, straight stretches between points fixed by hill-top signalling. Standing some 7 ft. high, it has two rods crossing each other at right angles and fastened in an iron stand by a pivot so as to turn horizontally: the sighting was by getting in line two plummet strings fastened on the ends of the rod and a distant object. The Romans also used a water-level (*libra aquaria*). But whatever scientific instruments were used, it must strike us as marvellous that the stretch laid out from London Bridge to Nonsuch Park would, if continued direct, have hit the East Gate of Chichester with absolute accuracy, as Capt. W. A. Grant perceived. The direct line, however, was abandoned at Ewell for reasons quite obvious to anyone who draws the line over a $\frac{1}{2}$-in. Bartholomew map and notes the contours and the nature of the ground.

The line of the road determined, the first task was to dig out side trenches, on the average 22 ft. Roman apart, as limits within which the road was to be pitched, and afterwards deepened into V-shaped ditches for drainage purposes. The site of the road was then excavated and filled with an appropriate bed; on which were laid the surface layers, the two together giving a depth of 10–12 in. in the middle of the camber. The metal was fixed by slightly raised kerbs of stone on either side and by pegs driven into the bed at intervals. In special cases the road would be supported laterally by a bank of earth. In its various lengths Stane Street, like all Roman roads, was adapted to the situations and materials available. In the many cuttings I have made through Stane Street it has always consisted of flints (gravel or from the chalk Downs) and pebbles, and in sand districts and in the Weald additional lumps of sandstone, ironstone and chert, and occasionally iron slag or cinders. Gravel pebbles for the 13 miles from London to Ewell were never far to fetch. From Chichester to Pulborough the South Downs could have supplied them without an excessive use of labour: and so on. For the various metals available for Stane Street see *op. cit.*, pp. 196–8. No part of this road was surfaced with stone slabs, although over the Yorkshire moors and elsewhere, where stone was plentiful, stone slabs were used. The nearest modern analogy to the construction of Stane Street and the generality of Roman roads is the Telford type, of a century ago. This has a heavy bottoming of stones of 4-in. gauge average, but sized to suit the camber, which was usually fairly high, but not to the 10 in. common in Stane

Street. The top was of 2-in. gauge, for which the Romans used mainly pebbles. Telford's, like the Roman roads, were not rolled in with heavy rollers, the consolidation of coatings being done by traffic. Like Telford, but unlike Macadam, the Roman used " fines " or earth to mix with the metal, and the rain had to bind the whole. Some Roman roads, however, had a pitched foundation of hand-set hard stones about 10 in. deep, with a coat of smaller ones, 3 in. or more deep. There is little doubt that such roads underwent frequent repairs, and when we find a buried Roman road, we find it as most recently set in order, if covered soon after disuse by a kindly blanket of soil; but very often it was stripped of its metal while it lay open, and so we find little more than the original trace.

Here is an example of road reparation made inside Alchester, a small town of c. 1200 ft. by 1000 ft., through which ran the Roman road Dorchester–Bicester. The results of excavation made by Mr. C. Hawkes in 1926 give a road, constructed c. A.D. 80–90, with a practicable surface 15 ft. wide, and another $5\frac{1}{2}$ ft. on either side underlying the steep camber—i.e., a total width at base of 26 ft. between ditches, which were $1\frac{1}{2}$ ft. deep and 3 ft. across. The original construction on gravel overlying clay was a laid core of stones, on top of which was a layer of gravel, with a surface of small cobbles in white gravel—the whole $1\frac{1}{8}$ ft. deep. The first repair was a 4-in. layer of gravel, and the second yet another of 6-in., the depth now 2 ft. 2 in. Last, a top stratum of gravel and surface of large cobbles give an extra foot; depth of the whole, with repairs, 3 ft. 2 in. Alchester itself probably came to an end c. 320, but the road through it may have continued in use, and the date of the last repair is doubtful. A very different construction was found by Mr. G. S. Bowes on Akeman Street near Asthall: here the road was built of flat slabs of local freestone, 1–2 ft. square, laid on the natural soil, supporting two layers of rough limestone (c. 1 in. × 6 in.), laid endwise and sloping in gravel, rough stones being rammed here and there into joints of the upper layer to keep all firm. In Gloucestershire a similar road construction was found. Here are two more types of construction. Watling Street, at Hartshill, east of Wellington (Salop), had on top a 6-in. layer of black concrete, over another 9–12 in. of sandstone resting on oak logs 8–12 in. diameter, laid across the road diagonally $4\frac{1}{2}$ ft. apart. Over the logs had been laid 3–4 in. of holly twigs, with moss and clay above them. The diagonal logs were found also in Wellington itself. The road across Blackstone Edge in Yorkshire built by Hadrian, and still visible in places, consisted mostly of large stone blocks trimmed square and set on edge. It is bounded by large stone kerbs

set 16 ft. apart and sunk deep in the ground. All this, according
to Mr. I. A. Richmond, was originally laid on solid peat, with only
a little gravel bedding to hold firm any blocks with uneven bases.
A peculiar feature here, found also in Cumberland and at Kenchester, is a series of larger stones running along the centre, and
helping to hold the others in position. Where the gradient is steep
these central stones have been worn into a deep groove: drivers
used them for the wheel of their vehicle which carried the skid
or iron shoe (*sufflamen*). Naturally such grooves would be worn
deeper, as they formed a water-course down the slopes. On the
level the central stones are hardly worn at all (I. A. Richmond,
Huddersfield in Roman Times).

The roads in different parts of Britain differed considerably in
character, and beside the Telford and stone-paved types, there
were high metalled embankments with a pronounced *agger* or
mound, for easier drainage in marshy places. Cuttings are often
made to mitigate an uphill gradient, and terraces are common
along the sides of slopes, as are causeways in marshy low ground,
as at Pulborough, Merton, and Street (Somerset).

After they had become derelict, the mounded roads served ad-
mirably as straight boundaries of parishes or counties; hedgerows,
either a natural product or planted, mark the course through many
miles of country.

Along Roman roads would be found at intervals *mansiones* or
rest stations, generally a day's journey apart. They represent
order, an official courier system, and links in a commercial chain.
Each *mansio* was a small defensible post, with bank and ditch, and
a gate at each end for the road, which ran through the centre.
It had quarters for the *mancipes*—semi-military policemen—who
controlled the road, accommodation for travellers and the *veredarii*
(postilions), stabling for their horses, and sheds for carts and
carriages maintained there for commercial messengers (*tabellarii*)
and ordinary travellers (*viatores*). Between *mansiones* were
mutationes—i.e., stages for change of horses—with a *taberna* for
refreshments. A typical *mansio* is Alfoldean (Sussex), excavated
by me in 1922–3, on Stane Street near where it crosses the Guildford road, north-west of Slinfold. It is one of four on this road,
the others being Hardham, near Pulborough, Dorking and Merton.
The station attracted a small population, which settled by the road
to the south. Like the three other stations, it is sited just south
of a stream, here the Arun. The western *vallum* and fosse are
quite clear today, though the ground has been under the plough
probably for centuries. Stane Street ran straight through the

entre, and crossed the Arun by a timber bridge. The station measured approximately 350 ft. × 310 ft. The H.Q. building with a stone-paved yard was close to the road on the east side, and the *taberna* or canteen, 26 ft. × 29 ft., nearly opposite it on the west. It had floor of rammed clay. There were indications of other buildings, a tessellated floor and a long wall, and remains of the guard house at the southern gate. Apparently it was in use between A.D. 70 and 350, perhaps with an interval between A.D. 180 and 350, when it was uninhabited. Much of the pottery was early, locally made, and showing Celtic influence.

Recently a Roman road through Surrey and Sussex was skilfully proved by the excavations of Mr. I. D. Margary, who was able to follow the clues provided by two or three isolated stretches. It may well be called " The Iron Way ". A good specimen of its construction, 40 yds. of iron-cinder concrete, is kept open by the Sussex Archaeological Trust, and may be seen parallel with the public footpath from Holtye to Hartfield, at the Holtye end. The known isolated stretches were at Edenbridge and along the Kent–Surrey boundary between Wickham Court (Addington) and Coldharbour Green above Titsey. The whole of its 44 miles has now been established. The chief clue was given in 1929, when Mr. Margary had photographed from the air some areas of Ashdown Forest. Photographs revealed lines absolutely straight and

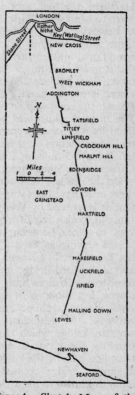

Fig. 4.—Sketch Map of the Newly Found " Iron Way ".

parallel, which on the ground proved to be shallow ditches 62 ft. apart and 4 ft. wide, with a raised causeway 18 ft. wide in the centre; between the causeway and the ditches were unmetalled strips. So he recognized an unknown remnant of Roman road, and the rest was a matter of persistence and skilled investigation. Here is the new

route. Its course southward begins at 77 Asylum Road, Peckham
where it branches from Kay Street (Watling Street), and goes b
Beckenham Station, West Wickham, the Kent–Surrey boundar
to Tatsfield, Limpsfield Chart, Crockham Hill, Edenbridge, Holty
Hartfield, the high ground of Ashdown Forest, and then by Fai
warp to Maresfield Park, Isfield, Barcombe Mills and Malling Dow
to Lewes; and so to Seaford. Its course and structure are typica
three long straights with changes of direction dictated by loca
conditions, and constructed with local metals as available.   Nea
the Roman iron mines in Sussex vast quantities of iron slag wer
used; flint, pebbles and rammed chalk near the Downs, and grave
where it was to hand.   Occasionally, as on the sand of Ashdow
Forest, the road was an earthen mound thinly surfaced with meta
The normal width was over 20 ft. and the camber 8 ins.   Apar
from its use for iron transport, this way through Andred's Fore
had no attraction, and probably went under soon after the Roman
left Britain, 3 miles at Edenbridge surviving in use much as did th
Causeway on Stane Street at Ockley.

On the roads, rivers were crossed by fords and bridges.   Of for
there must have been very many, though naturally few have survive
One is instanced by Ward, across the Trent at Littleborough nea
Lincoln, consisting of a pavement (18 ft. wide) of squared ston
kept in place between two rows of piles which had horizont
beams serving as kerbs.   Another similar ford, 20 ft. wide, too
the Roman road between Manchester and Ilkley across the Calde
and at Burford Bridge it was a ford[1] that took Stane Street acros
the Mole.   Bridges both of wood and stone are indicated at man
places, but remains of them are rare;   many an old bridge wit
semi-circular arch or arches is attributed to the Romans, qui
wrongly.   At Alfoldean I found distinct traces of the Roma
wooden bridge which carried Stane Street across the Arun: a
parently there was a masonry abutment on either bank, and
masonry pier in the middle of the river, to support the timbers
a similar bridge crossed the river Nen near Castor.   The be
remains known to me are those, still to be seen at Chollerford, of th
bridge over the North Tyne.   It had four spans, probably o
timber, resting on piers and large abutments of massive masonry
and measuring 184 ft. between abutments.   The piers were 31 f
long × 16 ft. wide, having cut-waters to the north, and the roadwa
was c. 21½ ft. wide.   A far longer bridge (462 ft.) was that over th
Tyne at Corbridge, with eleven waterways; its remains were ex
amined early in this century.   Instances have been found o

[1] Proved since 1936, the date of *With a Spade on Stane Street*.

medieval bridges into the structure of which had been incorporated portions of Roman piers and abutments: such was the case when the ancient bridge over the Tyne at Newcastle was demolished.

Milestones (*miliaria*) marked along main roads the Roman miles of 5,000 ft., so that thirteen Roman miles are approximately the equivalent of twelve English miles. A normal milestone was a cylindrical shaft *c*. 6 ft. high, inscribed with the name of the reigning emperor, the number of miles, M.P. (= *millia passum*), and the name of the place from which the miles are reckoned. Naturally they were sometimes replaced or re-inscribed. One found near Conway is inscribed:

IMP. CAES. TRAI
ANVS HADRIANVS
P. P. COS III
A KANOVIO
M. P. VIII

which is to be interpreted,

> The Emperor Caesar Trajan Hadrian, Father of his Country (Pater Patriae), Consul for the 3rd time; From Kanovium (Caerhun), 8 miles.

In the Leicester Museum is another which was inscribed:

IMP. CAES.
DIV. TRAIANI PARTH. F. DIV. NERV.
TRAIAN. HADRIAN. AVG. P. P. TRIB.
POT. COS. III A RATIS
II

Emperor Nerva, distance 2 miles from Ratae (Leicester).

But often they were rough, squarish stones, roughly inscribed. Several have been found in Cornwall, on which Mr. Collingwood has reported. Cornwall was little affected by the Roman occupation until *c*. 250, when the tin mines were taken over and worked as imperial property, and isolated roads were used for carrying lead from mining areas to convenient seaports. It is these roads, not a central road-system running through Cornwall and linking it up with the rest of Britain, which were marked by the rough stones of 3rd- and 4th-century types found at St. Hilary, Breage, Tintagel and Trethevey. The Tintagel specimen can be seen in Tintagel Church. The St. Hilary is a slab of local granite (or porphyry), *c*. 4½ ft. high, 20 ins. wide and 12 ins. thick, and is inscribed with

ten lines of rude letters 2–3 ft. high, which form abbreviations of the following:

Imp(eratore) Caes(are) Flav(io) Val(erio) Constantino Pio Nob(ile) Caes(are), Div Constanti Pii F(elicis) Aug(usti) Filio.

Set up in the reign of the Emperor Flavius Valerius Constantinus, Pious Noble Caesar, son of the divine (*i.e.* dead) Constantius Pius Augustus.

Constantine the Great was the son of Constantius Chlorus.

FIG. 5.—Milestone, St. Hilary, Cornwall (from *V.C.H.*, *Cornwall*).

1. The large Roman bath at Bath (built c. A.D. 55)

2. Bronze head of Hadrian, from the Thames

3. Plan of Roma
Villa at Southwick
Sussex, from the ai
The new road cu
through the Sout
side

4. Roman Villa c
East Cliff at Folk
stone, from the a

5. Theatre at Verulamium, looking
towards the stage and Watling Street

6. Milecastle on the West wall of Housesteads (Borcovicium)

7. Richborough. North Wall of Saxon shore fort, with ditches of earlier earth fort in foreground.

(*Ministry of Works photo—courtesy of H.M.S.O.*)

III

8. Portchester Saxon shore fort, with Norman keep in corner.

(*Ministry of Works photo—courtesy of H.M.S.O.*)

9. Relief of Mithras from Walbrook, London.

(*Courtesy of London Museum—by permission of H.M.S.O.*)

10. Ganymede pavement, Bignor

11. The Colchester Centurion. Inscription : Marcus Favonius Marci filius : Politus facilis centurio legionis XX. Verecundus et Novicius libentes posuerunt. Hic situs est.

(Courtesy of Colchester and Essex Museum)

12. Silver dish from Mileham, Norfolk

(British Museum)

13. Model of a potter's kiln

14. First Century " Face vases "

15. Roman Coins

(1) Claudius.   (2) Nero.   (3) Vespasian.   (4) Domitian.
(5) Trajan.   (6) Hadrian.   (7) Antoninus.   (8) Aurelius.
(9) Commodus.   (10) Septimius Severus.   (11) Constantius Chlorus.
(12) Constantinus I.   (13) Valentinian I.   (14) Theodosius I.

CHAPTER IV

TOWNS AND THEIR BUILDINGS

In Chapter III, while following the courses of roads, we have shown the geographical position of many towns of Roman Britain. Town life was the gift to this country of the Roman occupation and Roman influence, and its signal development was in the last quarter of the 1st century. The biggest and most important towns were the *coloniae* and *municipia*, both on the Italian model and possessing formal charters. Their citizens were *cives Romani*. *Coloniae* were either native towns to which a Roman status had been granted, or new towns on new sites, peopled chiefly by time-expired legionaries, auxiliaries or sailors of the fleet. A *municipium* was an influential native town which had been promoted to an urban constitution because of its big population or its high standard of Roman civilisation. Thus Verulamium was a *municipium* as early as A.D. 61, and included no veterans; but it was the only one of the five British *municipia* not established on military lines: the other four were Camulodunum (Colchester), Lindum (Lincoln), Glevum (Gloucester) and Eburacum (York). Military in origin, these towns did not flourish greatly: as Haverfield says, " We need not reckon very high the contribution of these towns to our picture of Romano-British civilization ".

More interesting and far more numerous were the towns of lesser legal status, tribal or cantonal capitals (*civitates*), whose names are partly determined by the names of the cantons they represented: thus Isca Dumnoniorum, Isca, capital of the tribe of the Dumnonii (Exeter), Venta Belgarum, market-town of the Belgae (Winchester), Venta Silurum, market-town of the Silures (Caerwent), Venta Icenorum (Caister-by-Norwich), Durovernum Cantiorum (Canterbury), Calleva Atrebatum (Silchester), Corinium Dobunorum (Cirencester), Viroconium Cornoviorum (Wroxeter), Ratae Coritanorum (Leicester), Isurium Brigantum (Aldborough) and Noviomagus Regnensium or Regnorum (Chichester). These, and many more like them, were the market-places and gathering centres of the natives of the cantonal districts, in which the old tribal system survived, though somewhat limited by Roman rule: the tribal *oppida* grew into towns with some sort of municipal privileges. The cantonal system preserved native institutions, but completely Romanized them. It was part of the Roman policy of denationalizing the provinces that the old native embanked

townships on hills were forcibly evacuated, and their inhabita
accommodated on nearby sites on lower ground, preferably by
river, " in peaceful places in civilized fashion among fat meadows
St. Catherine's Hill gave place to Winchester by the Itchen,

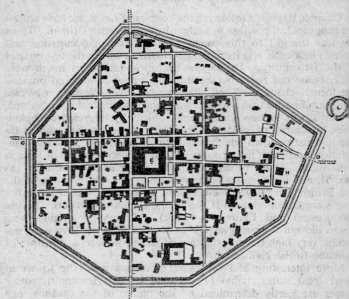

Fig. 6.—Plan of Calleva Atrebatum (Silchester), after the Society
of Antiquaries.

A, B, C, D   The Gates.
E   . . .   The Forum (with Church to S.E.).
F   . . .   Baths.
G   . . .   The Hostelry.
H   . . .   Temple.
L   . . .   The Amphitheatre.

Trundle to Chichester by the Lavant, Maiden Castle to Dorchest
by the Frome, and Bigbury to Canterbury by the Stour.

The new town life began and developed quickly in the time
Agricola (Ch. I, E). The new towns were laid out according
rectangular plans in chess-board fashion for the streets, thoug
the outlines formed by the walls are seldom rectangular—e.g

Silchester, Chichester, Canterbury, Bath and many others. Silchester walls form a nine-sided, Chichester an eleven-sided irregular polygon, and Canterbury was probably irregular in shape. The reason for this irregularity is sometimes that the area originally laid out by Roman surveyors in quadrangular sites for groups of houses had not been occupied up to its limits, and when the walls were erected (perhaps in the second half of the 3rd century) they followed the occupation line. The original plan of Silchester provided for a square within which were fifteen rectangular areas, called *insulae* (islands), the forum (market-place) occupying most of two near the centre. Each area is bounded by four streets, which are faced by some of the houses, the others standing obliquely and irregularly away from the streets inside the squares. After a time the plan was enlarged to about twice the original size, but all the space had not been built on when the walls were erected to enclose the built-up area: the population of this comfortable residential town administering the territory of the Atrebates was probably never more than 3000–4000. The lay-out of unused *insulae* has been found extending outside the walls. The four gates were at the four points of the compass, as they were at Caerwent, where there were about twenty *insulae*, with basilica (town-hall) and forum near the centre, but the whole within nearly rectangular limits, about 500 yds. east–west, and 400 yds. north–south.

All Roman-built towns in Britain were arranged on this plan of *insulae*. Chichester is another good example, Speed's map (*c.* 1610) showing quite clearly the plan of the *insulae* still existing, and the two main streets crossing in the centre, north–south 738 yds., east–west 773 yds. The medieval, sited almost on the Roman, walls enclose an irregular polygon of eleven sides, and contain *c.* 101 acres, much the same size and shape as Silchester: the complete circuit is 1 m. 810 yds. Walled Verulamium was twice the size. Chichester's amphitheatre was close outside the walls on the south-east side; Silchester's north-east, near the east gate. Incidentally, these two names, like Kenchester, show that " chester " often signifies simply a town of Roman origin, not necessarily the place of a Roman camp (*castra*).

Such towns were mostly small; London, which developed rapidly in early Roman times, was by far the biggest: apart from a suburb where Southwark now is, it eventually covered some 325 acres. It may be surprising, but, so far as is at present known, Cirencester was London's nearest rival, with 240 acres. Verulam had *c.* 200, Wroxeter 170, Colchester and Leicester a little over 100, Chichester and Silchester 100. Next in descending degrees are

Dorchester (Dorset), Aldborough, Lincoln, Caister-by-Norwich, Bath and Kenchester (Magnae) on the Wye, the last with only 17 acres. Of these Dorchester had walls on south and west of about 730 yds., at right angles, while the others, outside which runs the river, were more or less on an arc, so that the town occupied the quadrant of a circle, enclosing about 80 acres. One piece is still

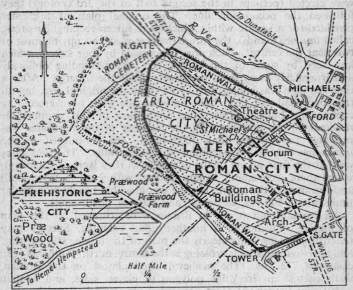

Fig. 7.—Verulamium, Prehistoric, Early Roman and Later Roman Cities. (Courtesy of *The Times*.)

visible at the upper end of West Walks, and the avenues planted between 1702 and 1743 follow the lines of the south and west walls. Outside the town, again, was the amphitheatre now known as Maumbury Rings, near the Cattle Market.

Godmanchester, 14 m. from Cambridge, by Roman road, was on the south of the Ouse, but there are no traces of surrounding walls or banks. It was probably bounded thus: west by Post Street, Causeway and Silver Street, south by London Street, east by Ermine Street, and north by East Street. There was a settlement also on the Huntingdon side of the river. The town grew up early at a river crossing on an early road. The enceinte of

Wroxeter (Viroconium) is exceptional as being curved, roughly pear-shaped, the broader curve towards the north, the Roman road to the north running through the centre and being joined inside the walls by Watling Street from the north-east. The modern village of Wroxeter is at the south extremity, and the basilica (town hall, law courts and exchange) and baths and forum in the centre of the Roman enclosure, the south-west portion of which impinges on the bank of the river Severn. Stretches of wall are still visible to the north-west and south-east. The treasures of this " White town in the Woodland " are in Shrewsbury Museum. The more regular chessboard plan is reasonably inferred from excavation for Exeter and Colchester, Wheeler's conjectural street-plan, worked out from the known position of five streets, for the latter giving forty squares, the larger part of two being allotted to a public building. An east–west street roadway was 12 ft. wide, and metalled in three layers to a depth of 3 ft. 9 ins. This rigid street system was due to the military surveyors who laid out the town on the vacant site after Boudicca's rebellion (Ch. I, D). In 1920 excavations due to the Morant Club discovered two houses (of an *insula*) entered from an east–west street, which we may take as fair samples of town houses. They consist of ranges of rooms flanked by corridors at right angles to the street, and both enclose central courtyards, as houses at Caerwent. The dimensions of this *insula* were *c.* 440 ft. × 290 ft., thus resembling the *insulae* adjoining the basilica at Wroxeter ; the largest regular *insula* at Silchester measured 390 ft. × 380 ft. (*Trans. Essex Arch. Soc.*).

Last let us think of Londinium. Phoenix-like the town rose from its ashes after Boudicca's rebellion ; it recovered rapidly, and, extending westward, soon enclosed *c.* 325 acres. The earliest Londinium was probably conterminous with the eastern half of " the City " of to-day, with a river frontage on the line of Lower Thames Street, from Cannon Street to the Keep of the Tower. Its west side was on the line Walbrook–Mansion House–Bank of England–northern end of Throgmorton Avenue ; its north and east sides were on the line of the northern ends of Old Broad Street and Bishopsgate, and parallel (on the inside) with Houndsditch and the Minories. It thus comprised within it Cannon Street, Eastcheap, Great Tower Street, Lombard Street, Fenchurch Street, Cornhill, Leadenhall Street, Aldgate, Threadneedle Street and Bishopsgate. A line from the Bank to the Tower was its greatest axis. Later Londinium added to this the west half of the City, centred east–west by the line Poultry, Cheapside, and Newgate Street. Here Upper Thames Street to about the west end of

Queen Victoria Street roughly represents the river front; the western boundary crossed Ludgate Hill, parallel (a little east) with Old Bailey; just north of the crossing of Newgate Street, passing through what was Christ's Hospital and is now the General Post Office, the boundary turned east to a point close east of the south end of Aldersgate Street; here it turned north of north-east to near Cripplegate, and thence ran east on the line of London Wall to the south side of Finsbury Circus. The town wall extended for over 3 miles, but outside of it were very few buildings, except in Southwark. There existed a forum, basilica, temples, public baths, a theatre, and an amphitheatre (perhaps outside Newgate). The basilica was c. 470 ft. long and 150 ft. wide, stretching from St. Michael's Alley on the west, across Gracechurch Street, to Whittington Avenue on the east. Cornhill cuts across the site at its north-west corner. The chessboard plan probably did not apply with much regularity to London, partly because it was seriously interfered with by some earlier lines of roads, such as Watling Street to Verulam, and by the Walbrook and other streams. London's wall is its best preserved and recorded antiquity. From a base 8½ ft. thick it rose to a height of 20 ft., with the battlements additional: the fosse outside, separated from the wall by a 10-ft. berm, was 10 ft. wide and 5 ft. deep, and later, outside this, as at Silchester, a second fosse was dug. The wall had a core of rough stone and white lime mortar, and was faced with regular courses of smallish dressed stones, bonded at intervals of about 3 ft. with two or three layers of red tiles carried right through the thickness. There were six gates, of which Newgate alone has given distinct traces. Later were added to the walls bastions of semi-circular or horse-shoe shape, not bonded into the wall. The still later south wall, along the river, was of another construction: founded on piles, over which were transversely laid timber balks, the wall was of ragstone and flint, with alternate layers of red and yellow tiles.

It is clear that the citizens lived comfortably. Though the streets were close packed, their gabled houses were detached, with narrow footways between. They imported Italian sculpture and crockery, Italian craftsmen laid their mosaic floors and painted their wall frescoes. They enjoyed imports of many kinds from Gaul, Germany and Italy—wine, oil, earthenware and bronze and glass goods. Religious cults most in vogue were those of Mithras and the Mother Goddesses, and here and there, probably, even in early days, was a Christian church. London remained essentially a walled city in Roman shape till the Great Fire of 1666.[1]

[1] Consult Wheeler's Report: see "Some Books" on p. 137.

Here are a few more names of the more important towns: rbiodunum (Old Sarum), Durobrivae (Castor) Luguvallium arlisle) and Corstopitum (Corbridge). To exemplify the smaller untry towns we may mention Caerwent, Yeovil, and Letocetum Vall in Staffs.). The size and walls of Caerwent were mentioned ove: it had its forum and basilica to the north of its area, a temple to e east of it, and, somewhat exceptionally, its amphitheatre inside the alls north-east of the forum. Remote from traffic, it " remained nall and hardly more than a village ", its largest limits being some · acres. Yeovil seems to have been a small town occupied in the h century and earlier. The remains are somewhat scattered, ut the Westlands estate has supplied most of the evidence— uildings, tessellated pavement, pottery and coins comprising a oard of c. A.D. 361: more than one Roman house was brought light in 1928 by Mr. Radford, and a fine cement bath and more ssellated floors. South of Yeovil (1½ m.) was found a villa in '53, in a field called Chesil, and east of the town were other finds ". In the Municipal Buildings is a museum displaying all e objects typical of Roman–British life. This little township as close to the Roman road Ilchester–Dorchester. Letocetum Vall) in Staffordshire was a small walled town which has been urtly excavated (see further V.C.H., Staffs., I). Finally, Great hesterford in the Cambridge region was a rectangular walled wn of 35 acres, outside of which to the east was a small temple a rising ground. As a military station in the middle of the 1st ntury it controlled the northern exits of the Stort–Essex Cam lley and traffic along the Icknield Way. When the walls were uilt is not known, but the series of coins found ranges from berius to Arcadius. A large collection of objects found by eville (1847), comprising 1st-century Samian ware, Castor ware, onzes, glass and ironware, is in the Audley End Museum.

The private dwelling-houses in such towns as Silchester and aerwent were like the country houses, not Italian, but Celtic in pe; sometimes purely of the corridor form, i.e., with rooms ranged off a corridor, or of courtyard type, i.e., rooms arranged a three sides of a court, or a combination of the two. The sup- osed inn near the south gate at Silchester has rooms along three des of a court, separated by a wall from which there is a fore-court, ith a system of baths in its south-east corner. Country houses ill be discussed in the next chapter (V).

The forum in a Roman town was much more than a market- ace: with its adjuncts of basilica, shops and baths " it was the ntre of civic life and movement, combining the functions of market, wn-hall, law courts, exchange and a gathering place where the

townsfolk discussed matters of mutual interest, settled points of
difference, gossiped and idled—where public notices were displayed
and games were often held and religious festivals celebrated.
was the rendezvous for all classes and for all purposes '' (Ward
About every eight days, and roughly corresponding with ou
Saturday, there would be held one of the public holidays fixed in th
calendar (*Feriae stativae*). On such a day to the forum ever
soul in the place at some hour of the day inevitably gravitate
In the forum colonnades, in the nearby narrow, cobble-pave
streets crowd in a noisy medley of merchants, lovers, decurion
market-women, local militiamen, lawyers and clients, countr
bumpkins, loafers, tricksters, doctors and patients, wagons, horse
dogs. At Silchester the forum, including basilica, porticoes an
shops, covered an oblong *c.* 315 ft. × 278 ft. Round the foru
space (142 ft. × 130 ft.) was an inner portico, then shops and room
probably two storeys, and then an outer portico. Right across th
west side was the long, rather narrow basilica, originally with a
apse at either end. Opposite to it, on the east side of the forum
was an imposing entrance, an arch *c.* 45 ft. wide. Other entranc
were on both north and south sides next to (east of) the basilic
This was 233 ft. × 58 ft., originally with a nave and two aisl
divided by Corinthian columns. The apses, later replaced by rec
angular spaces, contained the tribunals with raised floors an
marble-faced walls. There were entrances to it from the we
ends of the inner porticoes. Similarly divided, the basilica a
Wroxeter measured 229 ft. × 67 ft., and had a tribunal at one en
with entrance opposite. The forums and basilicas at Cirenceste
Chester and Lincoln were larger, and had massive buildings an
colonnades. At Leicester (Ratae) the forum was first made *c.* 120
130, and its basilica and other features were found in 1935: th
mysterious '' Jewry Wall '' which had so long been a puzzle turne
out to be the west wall of the basilica, through which was an arc
with steps leading down to the forum.

The public baths at Wroxeter occupied a space some thre
quarters of the length of the basilica, to which they were attache
immediately on the south side. The west portion of this spac
was a courtyard with peristyles or corridors on three sides, and entere
from the west by a passage from a street. On the north-east of th
baths area was a vaulted hall, entered from the basilica and servin
as undressing room (*apodyterium*), from which on the south or
entered a large warm chamber (*tepidarium*) which served as a loung
To the west of this were two hot-air bathrooms (*sudatoria*), with
temperature high enough to induce perspiration; and again we

of these were two big rooms with hot-water baths (*caldaria*), *i.e.*, tanks in which the bather plunged before returning to the *tepidarium* to cool off, and to the *frigidarium* to end up with a dip in cold water. He could then take exercise in the covered corridors or indulge in games in the courtyard. The heating in the baths, public or private, and in dwelling-houses was contrived from an underground cellar (hypocaust), on the floor of which were pillars (*c.* 2½ ft. high) supporting a cement floor (*c.* 9 in. thick) of the room above. Into

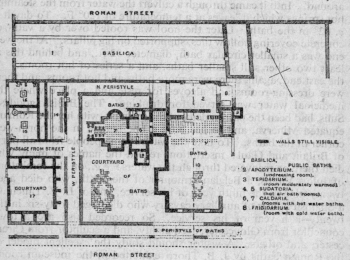

FIG. 8.—The Public Baths at Uriconium (Wroxeter).
(From Fox's *Guide*.)

the cellar space was pushed lighted fuel from an outside stoke-hole. The heat was not derived from the floor of the room, but from terracotta flue-pipes which, with open ends in the hypocaust, conducted the hot gases up the walls, into which the flues were sunk and plastered over. Ordinarily these flues are at intervals of a foot or two, but when great heat was required, as in *caldaria*, the whole wall surface was lined. The latrines in the Wroxeter baths were west of the western corridor.

Ex uno disce omnes: the principle was much the same in all public baths, though there was great variety in arrangement of the rooms. Examples were found at Silchester and Caerwent, and else-where. Baths were part of the attraction of the hostelry near the south gate at Silchester.

The baths at Aquae Sulis (Bath), erected soon after the Conquest on a site already in use for its hot springs among the elegant British, were as fine as any in Britain. Here the main feature was a big rectangular open-air swimming-pool, 80 ft. × 40 ft. and 6 ft. deep, having stone steps down to it and a roofed stone pavement around. Into it came through a culvert the water from the steaming hot springs—which it leaves at a temperature of 120° F. To-day it is c. 62° in the bath. Later the pool was roofed over by a vault of concrete covering hollow tiles, supported on big pillars. At the west end was a smaller circular bath, diameter 32 ft., and behind this at least two other still smaller baths, and a series of hot rooms. At the east end, again, there were more baths and hot rooms, and there were dressing-rooms and alcoves for rest, and a place where the medicinal water was served for drinking. The British goddess, Sulis, had been the patron deity of the springs: with her the Romans equated Minerva, and to her built a fine temple in the north-west corner of the baths. To take the waters came people from all parts of Britain and Gaul: inscriptions record the names of many who died there or recovered through the waters: e.g., on the tombstone of Julius Vitalis, a Belgian armourer of the XXth, who died aged twenty-nine in the ninth year of his service, and of L. V. Tancinus, a Spanish officer of auxiliary cavalry who died aged forty-six in the twenty-sixth year of his service. So recorded also are a town councillor from Gloucester, aged eighty, and a sculptor from Ciren-cester, and others. A visitor should study the excellent model of the Roman baths by J. B. Thorp exhibited in the museum room, and go through the big bronze door to the spring head. The tale of the gradual excavation of the baths is a long one, extending from 1755 to 1925, and especially through the years following 1878 with Major Davis directing. Consult *Catalogue of Roman Remains at Bath*, by Alfred J. Taylor (price 9*d.*).

From the delights and benefits of the Roman Turkish bath, we go over to the excitements of a variety show in the amphitheatre or theatre. The best-known amphitheatres are perhaps those of Dorchester (Maumbury Rings), Cirencester, Caerleon and Sil-chester, the last of which is now so badly overgrown as to puzzle the visitor. There are others at Chichester—a recent discovery—Richborough, Caerwent, Colchester, Wroxeter, Aldborough and elsewhere. All of these except that of Caerwent were close outside the Roman towns, and had excavated arenas, the upcast from which

rmed the surrounding banks. We may exemplify with Caerleon,
e external measurements of which were *c*. 267 ft. × 222 ft., and
the arena inside *c*. 200 ft. × 150 ft. The bank for the spectators
35 ft. wide was supported outside by a strong wall, and inside
its foot by a slighter wall. There were eight entrances to the
val arena, and seats on the bank. On the main axis north–south
e the two processional entrances, and on the minor axis two more;
d between each pair of these is another—eight in all. At a
rformance there was a "full house" of about 6,000 people in
is "diminutive Colosseum". Excavations were made in 1909
a Liverpool Committee, and again in 1926–7, when the *Daily
ail* bought the site for presentation to the nation and provided
rt of the excavation fund. As excavated, the amphitheatre is a
ational Monument in charge of H.M. Office of Works. Here
e structure, of date *c*. A.D. 80, was of stone over and outside the
rth bank; on the lower side the stone-work outside was preserved
a height of 10–12 ft. On the higher side of the original slope the
ating was in the scarped hillside, but on the lower the construction
f the wall preceded that of the bank. The masonry face looking
ver the arena was rendered with coloured cement; this smooth
rface prevented hunted animals from obtaining a foothold.
he floor of the arena at first consisted of the natural sand under-
ing the site. The building was extensively modified soon after
21 and again *c*. 212–222 ("The Caerleon Amphitheatre", Tessa V.
heeler, in *Arch. Cambrensis*).

The big Maumbury Rings at Dorchester (Dorset) had external
easurements of 345 ft. × 333 ft. and an arena *c*. 200 ft. × 180 ft.,
e floor of which was laid with gravel. At the south end was
enclosure opening to the arena and entered at the back by a
scending path from a south entrance; here the beasts were
ut up while waiting their turn at a performance.

The banks and hollow of the Chichester amphitheatre were
cognised in a field east of the Cattle Market as late as 1935;
at of Chester, quite built over, a little earlier. The Chichester
xample had a stone-built inner retaining wall, and an outer,
robably of timber. The entrances were at north-west and south-
ast, and the arena, *c*. 185 ft. × 150 ft., was floored with the natural
ravel. The inner wall, *c*. 10–12 ft. high, and built of flints and
ortar, was "plastered and painted in red, yellow, green and
urple on a white ground to resemble marble". Its date is *c*. A.D.
0–90. The site has now been built over, and has a road through it.
he Vandals could not find it in their hearts or purses to spare the
nly known Roman amphitheatre in the county of Sussex!

A Roman theatre in Britain is a *rara avis*; hence the comple
excavation in 1934 of the remains of one known to be in existen
under the soil at Verulamium (St. Albans) was of exception
interest. Mr. A. W. G. Lowther, who was in charge of excavation
came to the conclusion that the theatre was built originally abo
140, and reconstructed twice, in *c.* 180 and 200. It lay close we
of Watling Street, and was cut into the ground sloping towards th

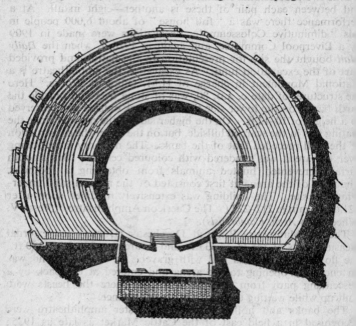

FIG. 9.—Verulamium Roman Theatre, *c.* 140 A.D. Reconstructed vie
from above. (Courtesy A. W. G. Lowther.)

Street. The tier of seats (*cavea*) rose like a great flight of curve
steps and embraced a circular arena for three-quarters of it
circumference, all open to the sky. The lowest row of seats wa
10 ft. above the arena floor, and so safe during bullfights and wild
beast hunts. Such use of a theatre orchestra was distinctly pro
vincial. The arena, 80 ft. in diameter, had two vaulted tunnel
leading down to it on opposite sides, passing below the bank o

ts, by which performers—men, horses, animals, chariots—
tered for spectacular displays. The small stage, comparatively
important, was raised some 5 ft. from the arena, its front edge
lowing the curving line of the arena wall. Behind it a compart-
nt long, narrow and high, contained the actors' dressing-rooms
d property-rooms; it had a lean-to roof sloping towards Watling
reet. The remains are kept open for public inspection (*The
man Theatre at Verulamium*, A. W. G. Lowther: the Marchand
ss).

The first Roman city at Verulamium was succeeded by a second
cted *c*. 150. The big permanent defences were a bank some
ft. wide, fronted by a flint-rubble wall bonded with brick, 10
man feet thick at the base: outside this was a berm 20–30 ft.
de, and then a deep, V-shaped ditch 80 ft. wide, with another
ft. wide at the south-west. The South (London) gate, through
ich went Watling Street, was a handsome structure 100 ft. across,
th double carriage and footways, like the Balkerne Gate at
olchester, which was 107 ft. across, with a projection of 30 ft.

CHAPTER V

THE COUNTRYSIDE: VILLAS, VILLAGES, AGRICULTURE

" VILLA " is the name given to a Roman–British country hou
whether a small farmstead or a big and handsome manor house
a large country estate. The word Villa, strictly speaking, mea
a system of land tenure. The Villa was an estate comprisi
house (*domus villica*) and grounds of a landed proprietor, far
buildings, granaries and dwellings for the dependents and se
(*coloni*) of the proprietor. The dwelling of the proprietor w
called *villa urbana*, the farmhouse the *villa rustica*. Large esta
were managed for the proprietor by a *procurator* (steward),
villicus (bailiff), and subordinate slaves. The *coloni* were not slav
but serfs attached to the soil. This villa system obtained in Brita
as in other Provinces; British *coloni* are mentioned in the Code
Theodosius.

Hundreds of villas (houses) have been found and excavat
in the lowland or more civilized zone of Britain. They cluster
thickly in the 3rd century in the north-west of Kent round Rochest
in West Sussex, especially on the coastal plain, and in Hants, in t
country on all sides of Bath, round Yeovil and Ilchester in Somers
to the north of Dorchester (Oxfordshire) and Alchester, and we
of Cirencester. Of the many that have been excavated and plann
—alas, very few have been kept open for public inspection
those that naturally suggest themselves are the well-known Che
worth, Woodchester, Bignor, Northleigh, Darenth, Folkesto
Brading, Angmering, Withington, Havant, Bramdean, Keynsha
Southwick, Ashtead, Box, and others. It will suffice to descri
two or three of these.

Four types are common: (i) the courtyard house, (ii) the corrid
house, (iii) a combination of the two and (iv) the columned ba
with rooms attached. Types i–iii were mainly one-storeye
resembling extensive bungalows: rather rarely we find a stairca
room leading to a second storey in a wing. (i) Northleigh (Oxo
is an example of a big courtyard villa. It is on the Evenlode strea
$\frac{1}{2}$ m. south from Akeman Street, and the site is now cared for
Oxford University. On three sides of a courtyard, an irregu
quadrilateral, are ranges of rooms. Along the north-west si
c. 240 ft. long, are the best rooms, some with mosaic floors a
hypocausts; these look out on to the courtyard and face south-ea
a very favourite aspect. The fourth or south-east side is enclos

78

by a wall, with a gate in the centre. During the three centuries of its existence it was rebuilt more than once in several parts, especially the central portion. Looking out from this on to the court, one would see the servants' quarters towards the end of the right wing. In similar cases the other wing was often used for industrial purposes or for the workshops necessary to the central establishment of a big farming estate. In all three blocks the rooms open out into pent-roofed corridors facing the courtyard. A house at Spoonly Wood, near Winchcombe (Glos.), is on the same plan, but simpler: all the rooms on one wing were heated by hypocausts. Many of the houses at Silchester are of the same type, though smaller. The rectangular courtyard is often completely shut in by four ranges of rooms, as in houses at Caerwent (see plan in Ward's *Roman Era*, pp. 76–80). (ii) A corridor house has no courtyard, and the corridor is its main feature, the rooms opening on to it; sometimes it is blocked at either end by a room extending beyond it and forming a rudimentary wing. The corridor, *c.* 8–10 ft. wide, is generally paved with inch-square red-brick tesserae, sometimes with a patch of mosaic. The plan of a house at Brislington, near Bristol, is given by Haverfield in *Roman Occupation* (p. 224). Very similar in plan is one of the villas at Mansfield Woodhouse (Notts).

(iii) Big courtyard houses are very often composite, with corridors both inside on the courtyard and on the outside—*e.g.*, Folkestone, below.

(iv) Humbler farmhouses are in the form of a big barn with two rows of timber posts supporting the roof, and so divided into a nave and two aisles. At either end, and sometimes inside the area of the barn, are rooms, with an occasional tessellated or mosaic floor and hypocausts (Plan, Haverfield, *Roman Occupation*, p. 227). A barn proper, situated near the Spoonly Wood villa, had two rows of posts, six in each, and was an oblong, 47 ft. × 28 ft.; thus resembling our big medieval barns.

The villa at Brading (I.o.W.) is somewhat out of the ordinary, in that on three sides of an irregularly shaped court there are three separate isolated buildings. On the north-west side, again facing south-east, is the main residence, with twelve rooms and the corridor outside—*i.e.*, away from the court. To the north-north-east of the court, from which it is separated by a roadway, is an oblong block measuring 140 ft. × 55 ft., tenanted probably by servants and retainers, and ending in a barn. Opposite this is apparently another barn with rooms attached. An interesting farm enclosure is that at Ditchley, Oxon, which had its well in front of the

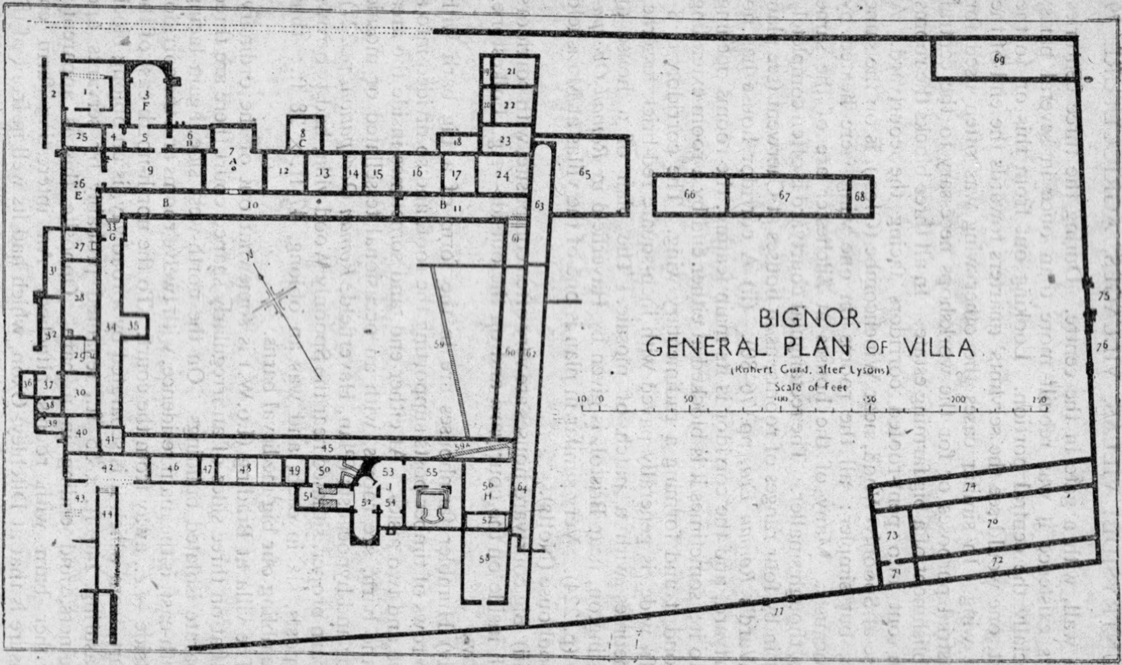

FIG. 10.—Plan of the Roman Villa at Bignor, Sussex. (Courtesy of the Oxford University Press.)

BIGNOR
GENERAL PLAN OF VILLA
(Robert Gurd, after Lysons)

Scale of Feet

neat two-winged house, a threshing floor, granaries, and other farm buildings.

With these chief types the reader will see to what extent a few of the well-known villas conform. Bignor Villa, near Bury, Sussex, is on a delightful site just below the Downs: it was excavated by Samuel Lysons early in the 19th century. Round the main court-yard there are sixty-five apartments, including corridors and divisions of them; the open side (east) consists of two ambulatories or corridors back to back, one looking outward to the farmyard. The chief residential block which contains the handsome mosaics is along the north side, the rooms opening off a corridor which continues round all four sides. To the east of the villa was a big farmyard of some $4\frac{1}{2}$ acres, bounded on all sides by walls, the eastern wall being pierced in the centre by a gate. At either end of this wall and inside it at the corner is a building, one of the big barn-and-room type as No. iv above. The villa is c. $\frac{1}{4}$ mile west of Stane Street, where, after its sharp descent from the Downs, it begins to negotiate the Weald, and was served by a branch road taking off from Stane Street about half-way down the descent.

To go into some detail. The inner court is c. 200 ft. × 114 ft. On the north side, no doubt suitably to the slope of the ground, the floor level is higher, and the best rooms are here, reconstructed c. A.D. 140; the system of baths is at the south-east corner, with cold plunge (still kept on view), and, in order westwards, warm room, hot room, and furnaces. The house probably of a wealthy Romanized Briton, it was built in the 1st century, and occupied till well on in the 4th century, when, perhaps in the great raid of Picts and Scots in 368 (Ch. I, M), it was not burnt, but simply deserted. The half-dozen fine mosaic pavements (preserved under roofs and shown to the public) rank in design and execution with the best in Britain—e.g., in London, Cirencester, Silchester and Woodchester—and the following description includes the main features of Roman–British mosaics in general. The *tesserae* vary in size from inch cubes of brick for the margins to very small ones of $\frac{1}{8}$ and $\frac{1}{6}$ in. on their exposed faces for fine work in the figures. The white are of hard (clunch) chalk, mostly for backgrounds, the red of brick, the buff of sandstone, and the blue and dark grey of limestone: a few of green glass were found in two of the pavements. This list is not exhaustive. In room 7 (see the plan), an apartment with a rect-angular alcove separated by curtains and used as the chief summer room, in the pavement is a six-sided *piscina* or water-basin (a feature not uncommon in Roman–British houses) c. 4 ft. diameter and $1\frac{1}{2}$ ft. deep. The mosaic of Ganymede and dancers represents an eagle carrying off the youthful Ganymede from Mt. Ida to Olympus to be Jove's cupbearer. Ganymede is in red Phrygian cap, red cloak and boots, and holds a shepherd's crook; the figure is enclosed by concentric circles of fret and guilloche (plaited rope) in colours, and a large saw pattern in black on white, resembling a circular saw, 7 ft. 5 in. over all. South of Ganymede and round the six sides of the *piscina*, were six hexagonal panels of Dancing Girls with veils containing green-glass *tesserae*. The panels were enclosed in a large circle 16 ft. 4 in. diameter flanked east and west by oblong panels of labyrinth; and there were vases, *cornuacopiae* (horns of plenty), leaf and flower patterns, and links in the spandrels.

The chief winter room was the well-warmed No. 3, with the *Venus and Gladiators* mosaic. In a circle the head of Venus has a nimbus as symbol of divinity and a chaplet of flowers, while dainty festoons supporting long-tailed pheasants lead up to the circle. Under this Venus apse is an oblong panel 14 ft. $\times$ 2 ft. 3 in., filled with winged Cupids playing the parts of gladiators in a training-school. A *rētiarius*, armed with his net (*rēte*), trident and short sword, is lightly clad in tunic and girdle. The *secūtor* (chaser) wears a helmet with vizor, a breast-plate, a greave on the left leg, and holds a curved shield and short sword. A retired gladiator is acting as instructor (*magister*), and holds his *rūdis*, or wand of office. There are twelve figures arranged in four groups. Left to right: *Secutor* and *Retiarius* fighting, *magister* as umpire. *Secutor* has disarmed *Retiarius*, but *magister* intervenes. *Secutor* is being armed, and *Retiarius* is being led into the fray. *Secutor*, having wounded *Retiarius*, is about to give him the *coup de grâce*. Two stones with rings are those to which prisoners of war, who often served as gladiators, were hobbled. In the south part of the mosaic were dancing Cupids in panels. (This pavement was relaid and restored in 1929.)

In room 6 is a geometrical pavement in good condition. In a central oblong is a vase out of which grow lotus flowers and heart-shaped leaves. The Roman quatrefoil here used is no doubt the parent of the medieval design. Interlaced links and guilloche are probably symbolical of fidelity. In corridor No. 10 is a patch of mosaic, and in room 26 is a much-admired figure of Winter, appropriately in the north-east corner of a pavement representing the Four Seasons, a common motive in mosaics. Symbolically he carries a bare bough over his left shoulder, and wears the British warm cloak mentioned in an edict of Diocletian in 301. The wintry effect is skilfully provided by the use of black, brown and blue-grey *tesserae*. The least artistic of the Bignor mosaics remaining is the Medusa in room 33: a lounge or dressing-room for the baths. Jealous Athena has turned Medusa's hair-tresses into snakes: the wave pattern, common in Roman mosaics, goes back to many

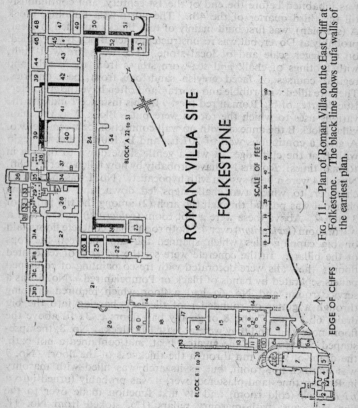

Fig. 11.—Plan of Roman Villa on the East Cliff at Folkestone. The black line shows tufa walls of the earliest plan.

ROMAN VILLA SITE
FOLKESTONE

centuries B.C. The Medusa device was regarded as an amulet against evil-eye.[1]

The Folkestone Villa (dug in 1924) is one of the few built on sea-cliffs. Its windows commanded an uninterrupted view across the Straits to Gessoriacum (Boulogne), and of the entrance to the

[1] See *Bignor Roman Villa*, Winbolt and Herbert (Oxford Press).

harbours of Dover and Folkestone. A watch on the cliff by *The Valiant Sailor* would have seen triremes entering the Port of Lympne (*Lemanis*), and could signal with semaphore in either direction. There was pre-Roman occupation of the site, but the Roman Villa was inhabited before the end of the 1st century, and continuously till the third quarter of the 4th. The north-west building, Block A (see plan), was first built mainly of tufa blocks quarried in Kent, probably at Dover, but was reconstructed, when Block B was added, on a bigger scale and of local stone. The walls are well built, with footings of chalk and sea-worn stones from the beach, and regular courses of faced greyish sandstone from local quarries. They are filled with rubble and mortar, and often have the characteristic courses of big Roman red tiles. In this instance I indicate the various uses to which the rooms were put. Block A is the main villa, Block B the annexe, with no wall connection between the two. A gives a continuous wall of 207 ft., and B, 180 ft. Let us begin with B at the cliff edge; it was a gentle slope down to the sea in Roman times. Rooms 1–5 have probably by now fallen over the cliff. Nos. 1–4 were a bath system with hypocaust. No. 1 was the stoking chamber, to which two chalk steps led down, and the glowing charcoal was pushed through the arch (2) among the tile pillars of 3 and 4. Above these were a hot room (*caldarium*) over 3, and a warm room (*tepidarium*) over 4. Both rooms had concrete floors laid on big capping tiles which spanned the gaps between the tops of the pillars. In the concrete were set the *tesserae* of tessellated floors; the walls were decorated with fresco painting of columned panels separated by bands of black or Pompeian red. No. 5 was a service room, and No. 6a had a floor which required draining through a gutter of rounded roof tiles, discharging into the big drain, 6b. Nos. 7 and 8 originally had floors *c.* $3\frac{1}{2}$ ft. above the floors now seen, and they were at least 1 ft. thick. No. 8, the apse-shaped chamber, had the greatest heat, and contained a hot bath, the drain of which ran through the thickness of the floor. No. 7 was another hot room, but as its arch was filled with masonry in Roman times and plastered over, it was probably turned into a *frigidarium* (cold room) and its first function made over to the fine hypocaust with masonry pillars (12), stoked from No. 11. No. 10 was a latrine discharging into the drain outside 8. No. 15 was a sitting-room, No. 16 a bedroom with space (17) around it, No. 18 a dining-room next to 19, a kitchen with two hearths. Nos. 13 and 14 were corridors, and opposite 15, in the outer wall of 14, was a pillared entrance. No. 20 was a yard outside the kitchen, and 21 probably a small garden.

Block A comprises Nos. 22–53; it looks south-east over the court. We begin with the south wing at no. 22, which is an *exhedra*—sitting-room with sea view—and a curtained-off alcove east of the two buttresses; it exactly corresponds to No. 51 in the north wing. No. 23 was perhaps a bedroom, 25 an office, 26 a staircase room leading to a storey over the wing, and 24 a long, uninterrupted corridor with an L turn. In 22, 25, 26 and 27 can be seen remains of the tufa walls of the earlier villa; they were allowed to remain below the floor level of the later one. Just inside the east wall of the long corridor (24) the foundations of the earlier corridor wall were traceable, and again to 51. No. 27 was in the earlier villa a hypocaust, but in the later a room with a floor 1 ft. 10 in. higher. No. 28 was in both periods a kitchen, but a fresh concrete floor was laid over the old one (very much burnt and covered with wood ash), and two new stone hearths erected; a platform was made to support a hot-water tank with fire under. The tank man also stoked the hypocaust chambers 29 and 30. Service rooms, 31–33, were connected with the cold plunge bath by two steps (36). No. 35 had a warm tub bath, and its wet floor drained off in the south-east corner. No. 34 was a passage from corridor to bath, and separated the smoky, hot kitchen (28) from the sitting- and bed-rooms (37–43). These all had tessellated floors, of coarse red *tesserae* at least, but No. 40 was the chief room, opposite the corridor entrance, as is shown by its 10 ft. square of fine geometrical mosaic. No. 45 is a passage, 38 another hypocaust built on the floor level of the earlier villa, and corridor 39, extending between 40 and 42, gave access to the rooms from the west. In it was found part of a red concrete floor a foot down under the tessellated floor of 40. Nos. 44, 46 and 48 were probably service- or bed-rooms, 47 another kitchen; and 49 a second staircase room corresponding to 26, and leading to a storey over the north wing. Blocking the corridor is the porter's lodge (50). In the earlier villa No. 51 had a bow window for a sea view, but this was superseded by a rectangular front like that of 22. Nos. 52 and 53 were perhaps bedrooms. Between the wings was a courtyard (54). The villa is kept open by the Folkestone Corporation, which provided the excavation fund.[1]

Perhaps the largest and most symmetrical villa in Britain was that at Woodchester (Glos.). It had two large courts, an inner and a larger outer, surrounded by buildings covering an area of 550 ft. by more than 300 ft. The western wall of the outer court is produced south, and along it were the farm buildings. As at Folkestone, the central hall of the north range has a mosaic pavement:

[1] See *Roman Folkestone*, S. E. Winbolt.

it is a fine specimen, 48 ft. 10 in. square, the best in Britain. The middle circle represents various kinds of beasts (as the Barton pavement at Cirencester), c. 4 ft. long, separated from each other by trees and flowers: originally twelve, ten have been identified as lion, tigress, stag, leopard, bear, gryphon, elephant, horse, boar and lioness. In an inner zone are a fox and birds, five of which have been distinguished—peacock, duck, dove, and hens and cock pheasant. The central design was an octagonal compartment, on the south side of which was Orpheus playing on his lyre; in the middle was a basin for water, as at Bignor. Orpheus occurs also at Brading (I.o.W.), at Cirencester (the Barton) and the big villa at Withington, near Cheltenham. At Woodchester eight other rooms and some corridors contained mosaic floors. Systematic excavation was made by S. Lysons in 1793.

These are but a few examples of villas. Reasons of space forbid further description of Chedworth (Glos.), which is kept open, the fine bath system at Angmering (Sussex), Atworth and Keynsham (Somerset), the bath system at Wiggonholt (Sussex), and many more. At Southwick (Sussex) there were baths on the east side of the court and in its north-west corner.

For Roman–British villages there is a rich region in the part of Dorset due west of Cranborne Chase, many of them revealed by the spade of Pitt-Rivers. I should like to lure some readers to the very interesting triangle, the apex of which is close north-east of Badbury Rings, and the two sides of which are the Roman road (Ackling Dyke) running north-east to Old Sarum and Silchester (The Portway), and a Roman road running north-west which probably joined the Old Sarum–Mendip road: the base of my triangle along the north is a line through Winklebury and Marleycombe Hill, c. 9 miles long: the two sides are each about 12 m. long. The terrain from south to north gradually rises roughly from an altitude of 300 ft. to 700 ft. Within these bounds are no fewer than fourteen Roman–British villages situated on the chalk, including in the North Pitt-Rivers' Rotherley, Woodcutts and Woodyates villages, the latter close North of Bokerly Dyke. Others are on Handley, Chettle and Horse Downs and Knook Down, near Heytesbury. You will find, besides, camps and barrows and dykes galore. Of the more complete Roman–British civilization there is only one solitary villa at Hemsworth in the south, close to the apex and near Badbury Rings. And even richer than this is the Wiltshire Downs country lying between Old Sarum on the south and Marlborough on the north—i.e., in the west angle made by the crossing of the Silchester–Old Sarum and Winchester–Cirencester Roman roads.

These two regions taken together are *par excellence* the home of the Roman–British villages, carrying on pre-Roman traditions of agriculture. There were small villages in Kent at Dartford, Swanscombe, Springhead and Ospringe, and at Dorchester and Bicester (Oxon.), the latter an enclosure of some 25 acres. Others were at Ilchester (Som.), Dorn (Worcs.) on the Fosse Way, Totterdown near Avebury, "Stockton Works", near Wiley, Market Overton (Leicestershire), Baydon (Wilts.), Hambledon (Bucks.) and Madeley (Staffs.). In all these the natives lived in their own British style, but adopted the material advantages of Roman pottery and ornaments, and often had warmed rooms. In the Yorkshire Pennines the natives continued to live in isolation in villages rather than in hill-forts, but adopted Roman pottery, coins, etc. They were very little influenced by town life. Still, they roamed less, for a more settled mode of life was forced on them by the census (*e.g.*, in *c.* 115), which made registration compulsory for taxation and army service.

At Hambledon (Bucks.) there appears to have been a scattered hamlet, nine buildings of which are known in the Thames Valley near by. A corn-merchant's establishment in connection with neighbouring agricultural settlements was excavated some twenty-five years ago. There were three houses enclosed by a wall; the chief, standing by itself, and measuring 96 ft. × 82 ft., had two corridors, a bath and tessellated pavements. The other two were large, barn-like buildings against or near the court walls; in one a later cottage with hypocaust had been built. There were found fourteen furnaces of flint and rammed chalk, some in the barn-like buildings, for drying corn, while others were in and outside the yard. This merchant collected corn from his neighbours, and, after drying it, carried it in barges down the Thames.

The poor peasants living in such villages seem to have lived independently of the large neighbouring villas, and in the chalk districts mentioned above were isolated. They enclosed their round mud huts within irregular ramparts and more irregular ditches, until Roman provincial fashions reached them, when they filled up their ditches, covered their walls with painted plaster, roofed their timbered houses with red tiles, and warmed rooms with queer-shaped hypocausts. They brought home coral-coloured Samian bowls from the nearest town. They raised corn in small quadrangular fields, pastured some sheep, and made pots in the old British style. To the market they took corn, wool and cloth woven by their women. The Roman–British countryman had also his day of sport, for which he was so skilled in training hounds that they were exported to Italy:

" divisa Britannia mittit
    Veloces, nostrique orbis venatibus aptos.''

(Distant Britain sends us swift hounds, useful for hunting in our region.)

The favourite quarry—*e.g.*, in the medieval forests of Charnwood and Sherwood—was the boar; but the stag and hare were both victims. All this is expressed in the altars dedicated to Silvanus and in the hunting scenes which ornament Castor pottery.

CHAPTER VI

PORTS, COASTAL FORTS, SIGNAL TOWERS

ROMAN warships and commercial freighters put into the following ports, among others. We begin in the north-east and go round to the north-west. The Firths of Tay and Forth (Bodotria), South Shields, mouths of the Tees and Humber, the Wash west of Brancaster, mouth of the Yare (Gariannus); the mouths of the Deben, Orwell and Stour and Colne (up to Colchester), the Blackwater for Chelmsford (Caesaromagus), the Thames up to London Bridge; the strait which makes an island of Thanet (Tanatus) between Reculver and Richborough, Dover, Folkestone and Lympne, Pevensey, the mouth of the Arun, which was at Heene, west of Worthing, Chichester and Portsmouth Harbours (Magnus Portus), the Medina (I.o.W.) up to Carisbrooke; Southampton Water up to Bitterne; the mouth of the Stour at Christchurch, Poole Harbour, Weymouth Bay, the mouth of the Axe at Seaton, the mouth of the Exe to Topsham, the Bristol Channel and Severn up to Gloucester (Glevum); the Taff to Cardiff, the river-mouth to Carmarthen (Maridunum), the Conway River to Kanovium, the Dee to Chester, the Ribble to Ribchester, the Esk at Ravenglass, and the Solway and Clyde (Clota) Firths. Of these the Forth, Tyne, Humber, Thames, Richborough, Dover, Lympne, Portsmouth Harbour, Southampton Water, the Exe, the Severn and Dee, Solway and Clyde were of major importance.

The Continental ports from which these were generally reached were probably Lugdunum on a mouth of the Rhine; either direct across to Brancaster on Wash, and so coasting to the Humber and the Tyne; or coasting along to Boulogne, Etaples on the Somme (Samara) and to the mouth of the Seine (Sequana). Sailings from Boulogne were to Richborough, Dover, Lympne, Chichester, Pevensey, Portsmouth and Southampton (Clausentum); and to the same ports from the Somme and Seine. Long crossings were probably taboo except in very favourable conditions; once across to Richborough or Dover, ships would coast north or south. The ports and forts of the south-east were therefore of the first importance.

In Chapter II brief mention was made of the forts of the Saxon Shore and their strategic purpose. In all cases these were probably ports before they were protected by forts. Into details of a few of these and also of the Yorkshire signal stations we now proceed. Whether Othona of the *Notitia* is Bradwell-on-Sea or Walton Castle (now washed away) near Felixstowe cannot yet be definitely decided: so says Miss M. V. Taylor, and on the evidences or want of them one must agree with her. Of Walton Castle the last remains had fallen with the cliff into the sea by 1754, but part of its cemetery still exists on the cliff. Drawings made c. 1623 show ruins on the cliff of one wall and round corner towers, and a ground plan of the fort as a rectangle with four external circular corner towers. The other claimant for Othona honours is Bradwell-on-Sea, where also the greater part of the fort has disappeared. The main argument, that Ythanceaster can be equated with Othona, is rejected by philologists: better arguments may some day be forthcoming. " The site of the fort was well chosen, close to the side of the Blackwater, but on the sea: it commands a wide view of all the coast to the south and south-east of Colchester." No doubt a creek gave anchorage. The fort was revealed by excavations made in 1864. Only a small part of the southern wall can now be seen, certainly of Roman construction. The 1864 plan gives a rough rectangle with rounded corners, the west wall measuring 522 ft., the remainder of the north wall 290 ft. and of the south 150 ft. The east part of the site is now in the sea. From the north-west corner and from the west wall projected two bastions, one semi-circular, the other horse-shoe shape, 16 ft. diameter. A gate is said to have existed in the west wall, where the Saxon-date chapel of St. Peter, now a barn, still stands; there were ditches outside the walls. The fort must have been linked by road with the London–Colchester road. Containing a little more than 6 acres, it was a smaller Brancaster. Probably a port already in the 2nd century, it became a defended port c. A.D. 300.

Possibly before A.D. 43, but certainly for nearly four centuries afterwards, Richborough (Rutupiae) was an important port for shipping, especially for the crossing from Boulogne, serving as a depot for stores of grain and other military necessities landed from the Continent, in the 4th century a base for landing troops and for the purposes of the fleet, and generally as the headquarters of the south-east defensive forces. The site was an island with sea on all sides, but on the west it was only a narrow channel full at high tide, and crossed to the mainland by a causeway, over which the traveller found the road to Canterbury (Durovernum). The island of Thanet rose to the north above the entrance to the channel going north to the Thames mouth at Reculver, west and south stretched the mainland. There was apparently a snug harbour behind the island to the north-west—i.e., north of the causeway. For many years recently the site has been under excavation for the Society of

Antiquaries (Low) and H.M. Office of Works, under the supervision of Mr. J. P. Bushe-Fox and others. A brief summary of results is published in *Richborough Castle*, the official guide (6*d.*).

The east side of the cliff, on the side of the Stour and the sea flats, has long ago fallen, carrying away walls and buildings. Here landed the Claudian expeditionary force, and defended itself by a double line of ditches, but the success of the invasion in the south and the midlands made unnecessary the maintenance of a fortified camp. Military and commercial affairs went on smoothly until the Saxon raids of the 3rd century compelled the construction of a fort defended by a series of three ditches and a stockaded mound of earth. But, this proving inadequate, its ditches were filled in and mound levelled, and a larger and stronger Saxon shore fort was built, of the massive walls of which we still see impressive remains. Outside the walls were two ditches, except on the southern stretch of the west side, where there were three. The fort is essentially like those of Brancaster, Portchester and others. This threefold development can be clearly traced in the earthworks, houses, etc., preserved on the site. The Saxon shore fort was rectangular, with walls (exterior) 494 ft. north–south, and *c.* 560 ft. east–west, the area enclosed being a little more than 6 acres. Walls seem rise to a maximum of 25 ft., and are *c.* 11 ft. thick. From the face of the wall rectangular towers projected *c.* 10 ft. The mainland entrance was in the west wall, 50 ft. north of the centre, and there was almost certainly a sea gate in the east wall. In the midst of the mid-3rd century defences is the great rectangular foundation which, with the cruciform base on it, is a mystery. Built to carry an enormous weight, it may have supported a huge pharos or light tower, or, more probably, an imposing Imperial monument commemorating the conquest of Britain. This foundation of big flints in mortar was sunk to 30 ft. in the soil, and at ground level measures 146 ft. × 106 ft. Centrally on it is the great cross, *c.* 4½ ft. high, the north and south arms measuring 8½ ft. wide and 46 ft. long, and east and west arms 22 ft. × 47 ft. But enough has been said, I hope, to induce visitors to make the 1½-m. journey from Sandwich to see for themselves and study the " finds " in the museum.

If it were not necessary to proceed by sample, details of Pevensey and Portchester should be included here. But we will now take a glimpse of three less-known sites—Lympne, Brancaster and Burgh Castle—the more firmly to establish the type. Lemanis (*ad Portum Lemanis, Ant. It.*) is Lympne in Kent. The Roman fort is now called Stutfall Castle, and is a good 1½ m. from the present sea

beach, but hardly ½ m. south of the village of Lympne. The sea wa
has gone, but of the others there are considerable remains extra
ordinarily tumbled about by landslides. The walls, which probabl
formed a pentagon of about 790 ft. × 660 ft., are very thick, wit
bastions of Pevensey type—*i.e.*, elongated sides and semi-circula
fronts. The principal gate was towards the south end of the ea
side, and there was a postern at the north salient, and two other
on the west side. The internal area was over 19 acres, accommoda
ing, according to Hyginus' estimate for permanent forts of *c.* 20
men to an acre, about 1800 men. The Roman harbour is sai
to have been at West Hythe, some ½ m. east of the fort and nov
1¼ m. from the sea, to which place runs the Roman road (Ston
Street) from Canterbury; but it is probable that the fort had it
own harbour right up to its walls, as had Portchester; for, a
Haverfield points out, the lowest fragments of the fort are on se
level, while the highest are 150 ft. above, and " the fort was obviousl
placed there on the slope in order to combine access to a harbou
with some slight elevation of general site ". Ships could reac
these walls before Romney Marsh was enclosed, drained and silte
up. Here, as at Dover, Folkestone and elsewhere, tiles were foun
inscribed with the initials of the Classis Britannica (Cl. Brit. o
Cl. Br.).

Brancaster (Branodunum), the most northerly of these fort:
and on a harbour of the north Norfolk coast, was a square o
570 ft., with an area of not quite 7½ acres. The concrete walls ar
11 ft. thick, and have facing and bonding courses of a local whit
sandstone. To the east gate there were flanking bastions; bu
there was an early feature—a small rectangular turret within th
rounded north-east corner. Previously occupied, the site wa
re-fortified in the late 3rd century. Some 4½ m. to the east is th
termination, on the shore at Holme, of the Peddars Way, a roa
which has no important Roman-British place on it, is obviousl
not directed to Brancaster and seems to have been made very earl
for purely strategical reasons, during the subjugation of the countr

On the river Waveney, close to its confluence with the Yare
one can row past the remains of Burgh Castle (Gariannonum)
Suffolk. " Yare " preserves the three first syllables—Garia—o
the name of the fort, but the existing mouth of the Yare is 3½ m
away. Quadrangular, but not quite rectangular, the fort measure
c. 650 ft. north–south, and 420 ft. east–west, and has an interna
area of 5½ acres. The walls, 9 ft. thick on foundations 12 ft. thick
are of flint concrete faced with dressed flints, bonded with tile
(three to a course) two deep in the structure, and the outer face i

etter made than the inner. The west wall, traced in 1859, but
ow nowhere visible, was founded on piles 1 ft. apart in the swampy
round. The pear-shaped external bastions were an afterthought,
s from their bases up to 7 ft. they are not bonded into the walls,
ough above that they formed one mass with the walls; they
ere probably founded on timber planking. There was a gate in
ie east wall and posterns in north and south walls, and there was
o ditch without the walls. The cemetery was outside the east
ate.

The fort of Reculver (Regulbium), in Kent, was sited on the west
de of the north entrance of the channel, of which Richborough
uarded the southern. The north wall has been washed away,
ad the remains are scanty, and building has been permitted inside
e area. According to Gough in his *Camden*, the fort was square,
ontaining 8 acres, and in his time much of the walls remained on
ree sides. The beach is still a happy hunting-ground for Roman
dicia—bricks, *tesserae*, *fibulae* and coins. At the time of the
uilding of the fort the first cohort of the Betasii from Lower Ger-
any was stationed there, whither it probably came from Ellen-
brough (Uxellodunum). The cohort was in Britain in the reigns
Trajan and Hadrian.

We will now take a glimpse at the signal stations of the Yorkshire
ast. The stretch of coast between Saltburn (north) and Filey
outh) is served by a picturesque coastal railway, so that the would-
investigator can reach the following objectives: Ravenscar,
arborough Castle, Flamborough Head and Carr Nase at Filey,
ing sites previously known or suspected. A fortlet at Huntcliff
ear Saltburn) was fully excavated in 1911–12, another at Golds-
rough (near Kettleness) in 1918, and a third at Scarborough in
19. Coast erosion has almost wiped out the remains of Hunt-
ff, so that some skill is required to find the site, but the finds are
the museum at Middlesbrough. At Goldsborough, however,
e easily reached site, being well up a slope away from the cliff
ge, has remained intact: it was found as the result of systematic
arch. It is well, then, to describe Goldsborough and Scarborough
representatives of the rest. For Goldsborough I draw from
e detailed account given in the *Archaeological Journal*, vol. 89,
the two excavators, W. Hornsby and J. D. Laverick.
The outer defence was a V-shaped ditch, 12 ft. wide and 4 ft.
ep, running all round, and crossed not by solid causeway, but
bridge. Between this and the outer wall of the courtyard was a
rm of 32 ft. The wall, 4 ft. thick, was built of roughly dressed
al sandstone, and enclosed a courtyard *c.* 104 ft. north–south,

and 103 ft. east–west, the four angles being boldly rounded a
having corner turrets of 10 ft. diameter, with projections main
internal. In the centre of the south wall was a gateway *c.* 10

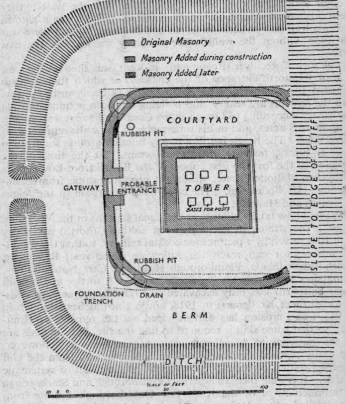

FIG. 12.—Roman Signal Tower at Scarborough (from A. Rowntre
History of Scarborough). The plan is very similar to that of Gol
borough, near Whitby.

wide, where the wall returned inwards for 6¼ ft., with a thickn
of 3 ft. 10 in., so that the passage was 10¼ ft. long. Stairw
3 ft. wide and parallel with the inner face of the wall gave acc

to the top of the returns. The courtyard inside the gate was un-paved, with sandy floor. To the south of it, between the wall and the central tower, was a row of eight open hearths of clay and big sandstones, and near the south-east turret was a well $8\frac{1}{2}$ ft. deep. The middle of the courtyard was occupied by a square building with sides 43 ft. long but internally $32\frac{1}{2}$ ft. long, the wall being over 5 ft. thick. It served as the base of a tower as much as 80–100 ft. high. The tower doorway was opposite the courtyard gate, and on its floor, arranged in two parallel lines north–south, were six large stones in the surface of which were socket-holes 10 in. square; they were probably the bases of stout posts support-ing the lowest of the wooden floors of the tower rooms used for living and look-out and signalling purposes. Access to them was by a staircase in the north-west corner, and in the south-east corner was a hearth. Cooking was done in two ovens cut out of the rock in the north berm. The garrison of some forty local militia-men ate pork, beef, venison, hares, rabbits, fish, crabs, mussels, limpets, whelks and winkles. The quarter-century life (c. 370–395) of the station had a sudden and violent end probably when Angles attacked during a Yorkshire coast mist or " fret ". Hadrian's Wall and the signal stations already abandoned, Northern Britain was now open to the marauding incursions of Pict and Scot, Jute and Saxon and Angle. The end was near.

Inside these stone walls was enacted a human tragedy, which shall be told in the words of the excavators. " In the south-east corner we made discoveries which can only be described as sensa-tional. A short, thick-set man had fallen across the smouldering fire of an open hearth, probably after having been stabbed in the back. His skeleton lay face downwards, the left hand, on which was a bronze ring, behind the back, the right touching the south wall. Another skeleton—that of a taller man—lay also face down-wards, near the feet of the first, his head pointing south-west. Beneath him was the skeleton of a large and powerful dog, its head against the man's throat, its paws across his shoulders—surely a grim record of a thrilling drama, perhaps the dog one of the de-fenders, the man an intruder."

Perhaps the most complete specimen known is that on Scar-borough Castle Hill, excavated by Mr. F. G. Simpson in 1922–1924. The east wall has gone over the cliff, but one may see much of the other walls, bastions and tower platform. Go in by the ordinary entrance to Scarborough Castle, and, leaving the keep on your right, make straight across the open field or castle yard to the bungalow on the cliff edge, south of which are the railed-in remains, well preserved by the Office of Works. V-shaped ditch, berm, wall, inner court and base of the tower are neatly turfed, and the lines of outer and inner walls marked out with stones. By ascending the tower you get an idea of possible lines of signals (see below) conveyed by smoke or flame. See the Roman pottery from the site in Scarborough Museum: it is definitely dated to the second half of the 4th century.

In 1921 Mr. Simpson revealed on Carr Nase, north limit of Filey Bay, the expected fosse, circuit and tower walls, etc. A Scarborough signal would be visible at Carr Nase, seven miles south, and Carr Nase would easily reach Flamborough, another eleven miles.

The Duke of Britain's instructions were, no doubt, to select sites from which there might be uninterrupted beacon lines coastwise in both directions and also into the interior.

Let us return to the Scarborough wooden tower and get an idea of possible signalling routes. A few miles west of Scarborough, Seamer Beacon stands out, an item in the system connecting Scarborough with the military centres of Malton and York. From Seamer the probable lines led across the flats of Pickering Vale to East Heslerton Wold; then round the north-west promontories of the wolds *via* West Heslerton Wold, Settrington Beacon, Grimston Brow, Birdsall Brow, Acklam Wold, the low hill west of Gate Helmsley, and so to York. From Settrington Beacon a signal would carry due west to Malton, and thence to York *via* High Hutton, Whitwell on the Hill, and the hill west of Bossall and east of Claxton.

CHAPTER VII

THE GOVERNMENT MACHINE

FROM the conquest to the 4th century, except for usurping emperors, Britain, an Imperial, not a Senatorial province, was under a Governor, whose official title was *Legatus Augusti* (Lieutenant of the Emperor), Pro-Praetore, and who was supreme military officer, in command of the army, the guardian of peace and order, the administrator of justice, and the regulator of the payment of taxes and of tribute in kind. As Britain had a garrison of more than one legion, the Governor was a man of consular rank, just retired from the office of Consul at Rome. The appointment was generally for three to five years. An officer commanding a legion was also a *legatus Augusti* (*legatus legionis*), but subordinate to the Governor. For the judicial side of his work the Governor had, at any rate for the period Vespasian to Severus, the help of a *legatus iuridicus*. (The change in military command made in the 4th century, by which the Count of Britain was at the head of a field army, has been mentioned in Chap. I, L. Here we may quote the *Notitia* for the similar official establishments of the Counts of Britain and of the Saxon Shore. Possibly one may imagine how much red-tape was employed. There was a chief officer from the chief office; a guard of foot in ordinary attendance; two auditors and a master of the prisons; a secretary; an assistant and under assistant; a registrar; and clerks of appeals, serjeants and other officers.) The imperial minister of finance was the Procurator, who, through subordinate officers (*publicani*), collected the taxes, and was much inferior in rank and power to the Governor, though the latter could not interfere with him in the discharge of his office: hence occasional friction, as in the case of Suetonius and the Procurator Classicianus (Ch. I, D). The Governor delegated local affairs to local councils. The centre of his government for religious, civil and financial affairs was probably London, in succession to Colchester, at any rate after the Boudiccan revolts; for the military side, York.

Local government, here as in other Provinces, was of three kinds, all of which have left traces in England.

(i) Municipalities, "burgess towns", including *municipia* and *coloniae*—privileged towns on Italian models. For the five of these known see Chap. IV. Each of them had a territory dependent on it, which may have been as large as an average English county.

The local government was in the hands of the Senate (*ordo*) of the town, with its officers: *duoviri*, *quinquennales*, *aediles*, *quaestores* and so on. We will return to details in regard to these presently.

After Caligula had given (211) the citizenship to every free-born subject of the Empire, all towns became in effect municipalities. There must have been many towns in Britain administering large territories, for the five chief towns mentioned could have administered an area of barely one-eighth of the civilized part of the province.

(ii) Throughout most of the rest of the non-military or Romanized area the cantonal system prevailed. As in Gaul, the administrative model for much in Britain, the unit was the territory of the old native tribe which had been governed by its king and nobles. To this tribal unit the Romans applied the government of their municipalities, making the nobles into officers with the same names and having much the same functions as the *duoviri*, etc., of the municipalities. Each cantonal *civitas* had as its centre of government the old tribal *oppidum*, or rather its Roman successor, either on or near the site of the old *oppidum*: Silchester (Calleva Atrebatum) was built inside the earthworks of the British township. In Chap. IV were quoted the names of *civitates* retaining the tribal names—*e.g.*, Isca Dumnoniorum (Exeter) and Venta Belgarum (Winchester). The merit of the cantonal system was that it preserved native institutions while giving them a completely Roman complexion. Some small places (*vici*) elected councillors (*vicani*) two *magistri* and two *aediles*. Old tribal aristocracies might, for the period of transition, retain a " king ", as the Regni of Chichester retained King Cogidubnus as Imperial Legatus. But such a *civitas* did not at first enjoy Roman, or even Latin rights. Smaller tribes were absorbed into new and larger units—*e.g.*, Canterbury (Durovernum Cantiacorum) centralized the East Kent tribes. The one *civitas* we are sure of in Wales is the *civitas* uniting the tribe of South Wales. This county council of the canton of Silure erected a monument (at Caerwent) to Paulinus, commander of the IInd at Caerleon.

(iii) Certain districts, including lead, tin and iron mines and stone quarries, were Imperial property. On pigs and ingots were pressed imperial stamps. But there were also probably big agricultural estates ranking as Imperial demesnes, managed by a procurator and farmed by *coloni*. Though there is not much definite evidence of this for Britain—*e.g.*, tiles stamped with Nero's name at Silchester—still, the existence here, as elsewhere, of Imperial estates cannot on general grounds be doubted. Pigs of lead sometimes have on them the names of the mine and of a private individual who had obtained a concession of mining rights.

Changes made in the government of Britain in the 4th century, and depending on the changes in " the government of the whole empire ", may be briefly summarised thus :

(i) The Legate of Augustus, Governor of Britain, whose office and title held for two and a half centuries—from the Conquest to the reign of Diocletian—is replaced by a Vicar of Britain, now one of the three dioceses under the Prefect of the Gauls. In the *Notitia* he is called *Vir spectabilis* (the Honourable).

(ii) Under the Vicar are four or five Presidents (*Praesides*), set over the Provinces into which Britain is now divided—Britannia Prima, Secunda, Maxima Caesariensis, Flavia Caesariensis and Valentia. The last was constituted after the others, being called Valentia after Valentinian I, who sent Theodosius to Britain in 369 (Ch. I, M). Of these five provinces the boundaries are unknown, though Prima probably comprised both London and Cirencester, Secunda Caerleon, Maxima Caesariensis may have centred in York, and Flavia and Valentia may have covered the western side of Britain. Valentia was probably not, as has been suggested, the territory between the two Walls.

(iii) The three military commanders appearing in the *Notitia* are the Count of Britain, of higher rank than the other two, who had general charge of the forces in the Province ; the Duke of Britain, who was responsible for the frontier defence in the north ; and the Count of the Saxon Shore, who guarded the south-east coast.

From this general sketch we now return to the functions of the municipal officers in towns like Verulamium or Eburacum : local government, section (i) above. Here the population consisted of three socially distinguished classes. First was the *Ordo* (Senatorius), *the* rank or order, the upper official class ; second, the *Seviri*, with functions mainly religious, and social status between the other two orders ; and third, the Commons, ordinary folk, exercising some electoral privileges and the right of appeal to the Governor and Emperor. The *Ordo* (or *centumviri*) officially comprised 100 members, rich and influential men of the town and its " county ". These hundred had seats on the municipal council, and were styled *decuriones*. Beyond these were others entitled to sit, and kept on a waiting list, styled *praetextati* (*i.e.*, wearing the *toga praetexta* of a juvenile), and being mostly the sons of *de-curiones*. This select body constituted a government of decidedly oligarchical character. The intermediate rank was that of the *seviri Augustales* (*seviri = sexviri*, six men), elected by decree of the *decuriones.* As the Sodales Augustales at Rome were a college of priests charged with the promotion of the worship of the Divine Augustus, so the municipal *seviri* or *ordo seviralium* were similarly responsible. They were largely freedmen, prosperous tradesmen who were " encouraged to place their wealth at the disposal of the community ". In time the office became a burden.

Of the Commons (*municipes*, if in a privileged town) there is little to say, except that they were entitled (at any rate in the early Empire) to vote as to which of the *decuriones* should hold the offices. For this purpose they were organized into voting units; otherwise they formed a corporation with separate official meetings, religious and festal. The commonest unit was the *curia*, or the tribe. The native population attached to the town paid it a *vectīgal* or tax, and if they had a quarrel with neighbours, they pleaded their case in the town courts. In cases of maladministration the commons had the formal right of appeal to Governor or Emperor. The officers were : *duoviri* (two), *aediles* (two) and *quaestores* (two), again six in all, elected annually. Groups of two are on the Roman check system—*e.g.*, of the two Consuls, two co-workers. A dictatorial magistrate might be controlled by his colleague's interference, *duovir* interposing against *duovir* and so on, and *duovirs* against *aediles* or *quaestors*, while these could not interpose against their superiors.

Highest in authority were the two *duoviri*—joint mayors, perhaps occupying one mayoral parlour—presidents of the council and chief magistrates for the administration of justice (*duoviri iuri dicundo*). Next were the two *aediles* (*aedes* = house), two surveyors, and so superintendents of buildings and public works. Their office dealt with temples, the theatre or amphitheatre, baths, aqueducts, sewers, roads, markets and taverns, and also regulated weights and measures. Even if not quite honorary, this office was, in the early Empire at any rate, apt to be an expensive one for the holder, from whom his fellow-citizens expected a gift of some public-utility building. This always being the first public office held, his public spirit had to stand this test before he could be exalted to the duovirate. Third came the two *quaestores* (*quaero* = seek after), revenue officers whose business was the collection of public moneys and control of revenue and expenditure of the colony. Quaestors had to account to the Ordo for their handling of public moneys. What were the revenues? They were mostly from public lands; from fisheries, mines and harbour-dues, dues on goods brought by land, fines, honoraria paid by new *decurions* and officials, rents from shops and other buildings owned by the town, and a water rate. Local taxation was comparatively light.

This gradation of offices was the normal, but in every fifth year, instead of the *duoviri* there were elected by the *decuriones* for one year special *duoviri quinquennales* (fifth-year mayors). Like the censors in Republican Rome, they were charged with the duty of checking the administration of the four-year period just past. They took the census of the town and territory, audited the accounts for the period, inspected public works, and arranged contracts for repairs and new constructions. If these were really independent men, their work must have been highly salutary in checking such abuses and jobbery as have been known to prevail in town councils. These six officers were elected from the body of the Ordo by popular vote; but admission into the Ordo was strictly guarded. When a new list was made every five years, first on it were the old *decuriones*, next magistrates sitting in virtue of their office, then rich citizens, and finally *patroni*, who were influential Romans. There was a big disqualifying list of undesirables— actors, exiles, gladiators, petty tradesmen, undertakers, bankrupts, notoriously immoral persons, soldiers expelled from the army, convicts and others. A *decurio* had to possess high property qualifications, in some towns roughly the equivalent of £1000, and when elected he had to pay a handsome footing fee. Honorary *decuriones*, called *patroni*, were sometimes elected—influential persons who might be able to put in a good word for the town. The Ordo was also recruited by co-optation of men who had not served a magistracy. The list of Ordo members was called the *Album*. A *duovir* could be re-elected only after an interval of five years.

How did these administration arrangements operate? Unfortunately, not well. By the middle of the 2nd century there was already a marked decline. Popular election began to be superseded, the retiring magistrates nominating the exact number of magistrates required, confined to the Ordo. Financial disorders had often to be corrected by *curatores*—Imperial commissioners—and such bureaucratic interference gradually " assumed the character of a permanent institution. The municipality thus became one of the thousands of units directly controlled by the State." Moreover, there were often hot disputes between the Commons and the Ordo, against whom the charge of avarice was hurled, and over whom the Commons had no control beyond the very indirect control of the vote for offices. " These *decuriones* formed a town council with more power and less responsibility than town councils as we know them "

(Arnold). Another way in which the central gradually encroached on the town government was this: the Emperor, elected as first magistrate, appointed a *prefect* to represent him and rule unchecked by a colleague. As time went on, and " as the system decayed, the possession of wealth was the one thing sought for ".

Inscriptions at York testify to this municipal structure. An altar was raised to the Divine Majesty of Augustus by the Ordo; a young *decurio*, Flavius Bellator, is commemorated on a sarcophagus; *seviri* and their families are recorded; Marcus Aurelius Lunaris was *Sevir Augustalis* of both Eburacum and Lindum— inscription dated 237 (*Roman York*, Gordon Home).

Taxes in relation to townships were noted above. We now take a more general view of taxation. Under the Early Empire in Britain, as elsewhere, the land-tax raised most money for the Central Government. Let us consider the payments which would be made by inhabitants—*e.g.*, of Calleva (Silchester). The private owner, the township as a corporation, the tenant of State property would have to pay according to the acreage of ploughland, pastures or forests; or the *annona militaris*, payment in kind, would be exacted and applied to maintenance of soldiers and officials in the province. Besides this the inhabitants paid an income tax levied on trades; merchants on the whole of their movable property—ships, slaves, horses, etc.—and artisans and shopkeepers (hosiers, weavers, goldsmiths and so on) on their earnings. Nor were the *coloni* or farm labourers of the Callevan territory exempt: they paid a poll-tax. The State-property tenants held parts of the general Imperial domains (*loca fiscalia*), or of the Emperor's own private properties (*patrimonium Caesaris*); in either case the land held was classed either as arable, pasture or mines, and managed by an Imperial bailiff called procurator (to be distinguished from the Procurator of the province). As the iron in Noricum or Gallia Lugdunensis, so the lead and tin in Britain were Imperial property. Next, our Callevan must pay a legacy duty of 5 per cent., increased to 10 per cent. by Caracalla, who exacted this from provincials in return for his gift of the Roman franchise. Then there were, among indirect taxes, the customs duties (*portoria*). All imports to and exports from Gaul, sent from or received at the port of Clausentum (Southampton), were dealt with at a customs port on the Gallic coast and paid 2½ per cent. on the value of the goods. But by the 4th century this had increased to the ruinous rate of 12½. Another indirect tax probably payable was 1 per cent. on all purchases (*centesima rerum venalium*), and 4 per cent. on purchases of slaves. The expenses of administration in Britain, however, absorbed all ιe revenues taken from it. After Diocletian the *coloni* were the ιief payers of the poll-tax, through the landlords who collected om them. But in the later Empire the really crushing burden was ιe land-tax. "It was this which made slaves of the municipal ιagistrates" (see Arnold's *Roman Provincial Administration*).

The cost of the conquest of Britain, its annexation and administra-on had to be paid by its inhabitants. "There can be no peace mong nations without arms, no arms without pay, no pay without ibute", is the justification of Roman rule offered by Cerialis (Ch. D). People who could not pay were conscripted to serve in the nperial armies. Tribute, soldiers and Roman law were the three hief ingredients of Roman rule. Soon after the Conquest a omplete land survey of the civilized regions of Britain was, we may uppose, made by the surveyors (*agrimensores*); that made, it was ossible for the *censitor* to take a census, and thereafter a fresh ensus was taken every five years, as in the town.

CHAPTER VIII

RELIGION: DEITIES, TEMPLES, BURIALS, ETC.

Of the religious beliefs and superstitions which prevailed in Britai during the Roman occupation we have much information, especiall from the great number of altars, cemeteries and tombstones pre served in the country. Deities worshipped are of four main types pre-Roman indigenous Celtic, Roman Celtic imported mainly b the army of occupation, Graeco–Roman, and Eastern cults receive in Rome and diffused throughout the Empire, including Christianity Which deities of the first two types were indigenous and whic imported it is possible to conjecture with some certainty; but, bot sides being hospitably tolerant, they were all too soon identifie with the most similar gods and goddesses of the Graeco–Roma pantheon. Soldiers levied in Britain or other provinces officiall recognized the Roman State gods—Jupiter, Mars, Minerva, Apoll Hercules and so on—and at the same time raised altars to thei own native gods, often under combined Roman and native titles— *e.g.*, Jupiter Tanarus, a German god of thunder; Jupiter Osiru the nocturnal sun; Sulis Minerva, patroness of the hot spring at Bath, and Mars Belatucadrus in North Britain. The variety c worships was great; Britain was, says Collingwood, "a land fertil in petty local godlings". It might surprise some, but the fac is that in this blend of religious cults it is the Celtic which graduall prevails. Of the official cults recognized by the military, the mos important was the worship of Jupiter: he was "the symbol of th *raj*".

An interesting instance of the worship of the purely Roma Jupiter in the 4th century is the inscription on three sides of a column base found in Cirencester, recording that L. Septimus, Presiden of Britannia Prima, restored and dedicated to Jove a statue an column set up in the old religion—*i.e.*, paganism—probably therefore, under the Emperor Julian (360–363), who apostatize from Christianity to paganism. Fortuna (Good Luck) was a ver popular deity, representing success of many kinds, from battle i the field to gaming in a lounge of the public baths; with her i often associated Bonus Eventus (Good Result). Those who ha arrived by ship and those who occupied their business in grea waters, even down to boat-builders in a harbour, prayed for th special protection of Neptune or Ocean. In illness one made vow to Aesculapius, the Healer, or his daughter Salus (Fitness).

This polytheistic miscellany, however, failed really to satisfy, in mind or heart, the consciousness of unity effected by Roman peace and culture. By soldiers and natives alike a warm welcome was given to new monotheistic cults derived from the East, which both attracted by their content of mysticism and promised satisfaction to such penitents as would expiate their sins by reformed lives as well as by offerings. Of these cults Mithraism was by far the most popular, at any rate among the soldiers on the frontiers; and strong rivals were the worship of the Great Mother of Phrygia, of Isis of Egypt, and of Serapis. To the last was dedicated a temple at York: Deo Sancto Serapi Templum a solo fecit Cl. Hieronymianus leg. leg. VI. Vic.—To the Holy God Serapis Cl. Hieronymianus, Legate of the sixth legion, the Victorious, erected the temple from the ground. These and similar oriental cults gradually prepared the way for the acceptance of Christianity (also from the East), which from small and early beginnings here of about the 2nd century gradually increased its hold, and was firmly established in the 4th and 5th centuries, though the legions do not seem to have changed much from their old faiths. At Corbridge on Tyne, pre-eminently a military centre, we find altars set up to a great variety of deities, among others to Astarte (Ashtoreth), Hercules of Tyre, Dolichenus, Sol Invictus, Panthea, British Brigantia, Maponus and the German Veten, but no recognition of Christianity.

To come to closer quarters. Inscriptions on altars to Jupiter begin with the abbreviations I.o.M.—Iovi Optimo Maximo (to Jupiter, the Best and the Greatest). Minerva had a temple at Ribchester, and she was also honoured in conjunction with Hercules and Neptune. A well-known example of a temple to Neptune and Minerva was at Chichester, the dedicatory inscription to which can be seen outside the Town Hall. In translation it runs: " To Neptune and Minerva this temple is dedicated on behalf of the safety of the Divine House, on the authority of Tiberius Claudius Cogidubnus, King and Legate of Augustus in Britain, by the Guild of (? Ship-)Wrights and its associate members from their own contributions, the site being presented by (Clem)ens, son of Pudentinus." The dedication to Neptune, god of the sea, and Minerva, goddess of handicraft, suggests a society of ship-builders, with workshops near by at the head of Chichester Harbour.

To the common soldier Mars made a living appeal. In the military districts altars to, and statues of Mars are naturally many, generally in a specified capacity as Conqueror, or Preserver, and he is often associated with Victory. Of a silver statue to Victory

c. 2 ft. high, part was found, bearing a silver plate inscribed:
Victoriae Leg. VI Vic. Val. Rufus, V.S.L.M. (=votum solvit
libens merito)—To the Victory of the sixth legion Victorious,
Valerius Rufus duly and gladly performed his vow. This comes
from Butterworth, near Rochdale, Lancs. In the bath-house at
Slack (Yorks) was an altar inscribed (trans.): Sacred to Fortune:
Gaius Antonius Modestus, a Centurion of the VIth legion Victorious,
Loyal and Faithful, paid his vow. We may suppose that, the fickle
goddess abetting, he had " struck it rich ".

Many altars are dedicated to the Genius (Guardian Spirit) of
the Roman People, of Britain, of the Emperor, and of the Place
(Genio Loci), as at Clifton, Cumberland (1847), to the Genius of
Brocavum: I.O.M., Genio Loci Brocavensis Septimius Apolli-
naris Princeps Centuriae. The Genius is a Roman, not a Celtic
conception. The divinity of the Emperor is often invoked, as on
an altar, dated 205, found in 1597 at Greetland in the Calder
valley (Yorks): the expanded inscription reads, Deae Victoriae
Brigantiae et Numinibus Augustorum Titus Aurelius Aurelianus
dono dat pro se et suis, S—— Magistro Sacrorum: Antonino II et
Geta consulibus. (To the Goddess of Victory of the Brigantian
territory and to the Divinities of the Emperors, Titus A.A. gives
this altar as a gift for himself and his family, S—— being in charge
of the sacred rites, in the second consulship of Antoninus and the
first of Geta.) In the Huddersfield Museum is another altar to
the God Bregans and the Divinity of the Emperor.

Among rural divinities were Water Nymphs, Field Nymphs,
Mountain Gods, and Silvanus, God of Woods and Wilds, the
hunter's favourite: thus Deo Silvano Cocidio Qu. Florius Maternius
Praef. Coh. I. Tung, v.l.s.m., Maternius being Prefect of the first
cohort of the Tungrians. Mars in British guise may be Belatucadrus
(the shining one), Cocidius, especially along the Wall, Louectius,
Rigisamus (most royal), Camulus, Ocelus, Condate, Toutates, or
Thinesus. Apollo Grannos, from Germany, was the patron of
healing waters. A Celtic Apollo was Maponus (the young hero),
much worshipped in the north, and the Mabon of Welsh Arthurian
legend. There were gods to protect from the risks of the road:
thus in Herefordshire was found an altar to the *deo trivii*—god of the
cross-roads—as it were to a modern A.A. or R.A.C. man. And
(in Yorks) a *deus qui vias et semitas commentus est*, the god who
devised ways and paths. Today we desire a god to preserve them.
Eponus and Epona, interested in horses, were the favourite deities
of the jockey and the charioteer. Mogon, who appears in the
north, gave his name to Moguntiacum, Mainz in Germany.

Coventina, a local (the Wall) water goddess, is represented as attended by a nymph or reclining on a water-lily. In the centre of her temple was a rectangular well into which flowed the water of a spring. Into it, as into medieval and modern fountains, were thrown coins and trinkets as offerings by those who craved her favours. The nymph or tutelary goddess Brigantia had altars found at Chester and London. The Romanized Lludd had a shrine at Lydney on Severn. Among other gods are Antenociticus and

FIG. 13.—The Mother Goddesses.

Matunus (the kindly one), and among goddesses Ancasta, Harinella and others. There was an important trinity of goddesses, the Deae Matres, Mother goddesses, to whom over thirty altars and inscriptions have been found, three of the altars being in York Museum. They are represented as three young women seated, and dressed in long robes, holding in their laps baskets of fruit. They are peculiarly imported, "transmarine", introduced here by the soldiers, as protectors of fields, cities and nations. They came here from Cisalpine Gaul via the Rhineland. At Walton (Northumberland) was a temple to them as Mothers of all Nations. Three goddesses resembling them, and called Suleviae, had altars erected to them at Colchester, Cirencester and Bath. A single Great Mother, the Syrian goddess, was worshipped as Producer

of Corn, Inventress of Sight, Foundress of Cities, Peace and Virtue
she has been found at Carvoran and possibly at Chester (th
Wall).

Mithraism, the worship of the ancient Zoroastrian Sun God o
Persia, established in Rome in the 1st century, came to Britain i
the 2nd, became the cult of cults in the 3rd, and maintained its hol

DEO SOLI IN VICTO MI

FIG. 14.—Mithras (from the Louvre).

till the 4th. In art Mithras, young and heroic like Maponus
somewhat resembles Apollo, but is clad in Phrygian costume and
cap. In the sculptures of his shrines—in caves natural or artificia
—he is represented in a cave, kneeling, with cloak flying back, on a
prostrate bull, into whose neck he has driven a dagger: this is the
mystic sacrifice made so that all other animals might be born and
renew their lives out of his blood. A dog is licking the blood from
the wound. Of two male attendants one holds an upright, the other
a reversed torch, symbolic of summer and winter, light and darkness

e spirits of good and evil. Mithras is revered as "Lord and
reator of all things", "Father and Source of all life". His
orship was a "mystery" because his votaries were persuaded
at this faith was revealed only to a select few: for initiation one
d to undergo a series of tests, like those of hunger, thirst and
litude. A well-preserved bull slab was found at York (1747),
d another at London, but perhaps the best examples are in the
aris Louvre and at the British Museum; another is at Arles.
emples or caves have been found at Housesteads (the Wall),
urham (Kent) and elsewhere. On altars are inscribed the words,
eo Soli Invicto Mitrae Seculari—To the Sun, the Invincible God,
ithras, Lord of the Ages.

Of British Christianity in early days there are very few evidences.
arly writers have stated that there were in Britain hundreds of
artyrs like Alban of Verulam and Angulus, Bishop of London,
 the persecution of Diocletian (284–305). Constantius Chlorus
lerated Christianity in Britain. Constantine (Ch. I, L) became a
eliever in Christ in 312, issued the edict of Milan in 313, made
hristianity the religion of the Empire in 323, and was baptized
 his deathbed in 337. Tertullian states (c. 208) that parts of
itain were subject to Christ, and Origen (c. 230) confirms this;
d in the 4th century bishops from London, York and Lincoln
ok seats at the ecclesiastical council of Arles (314) and others
presented Britain at Ariminum (360). The faith and discipline
 the British Church are commended. At the close of the 4th
ntury Britain produced Pelagius and his so-called "heresy"
h. I, P). In the 5th and 6th centuries Christianity is found existing
 regions of Britain where the English conquest was not effective.
ccording to Bede the church of St. Martin at Canterbury was
built while the Romans were still in the island". The greatest
ogress was made, as usual, among the poor in the cities, and
nong the less Romanized classes, the least in the military zones.
ery few are the certain Christian remains found. The Christian
urch at Silchester was a very small building, but was in an im-
ortant central position. The Chi-Rho, a symbol of the Faith
 using the two first letters of the name Christus in Greek, figured
 a mosaic pavement near Frampton (Dorset), scratched in masonry
 the villa at Chedworth, and on the pewter vessels of wealthier folk
s found near Andover, Hants). Ingots of pewter, stamped
ficially with the Chi-Rho and some with the motto Spes in Deo,
ere found in the Thames near Battersea Bridge: these are in the
ritish and York Museums. A Chi-Rho is a combination of the
vo first letters of the Greek word ΧΡΙΣΤΟΣ. The same

Christian sign occurs on a lead seal from Silchester (in Readi...
Museum) and on two small terracotta lamps at Guildhall, a...
some at York; and on a lead water cistern recently found ...
Wiggonholt, Sussex. Finally, the fish, a rebus for ΙΧΘΥΣ (Jes...
Christ, Son of God, Saviour), and so a common Christian symb...
is made in the form of a brooch (London Museum); exampl...
were found at Rotherley and Silchester. There are a few Christi...
sepulchral inscriptions—*e.g.*, at Carlisle, Lincoln and elsewher...
one at York has: Soror ave, vivas in Deo. Finally, a few coi...
have Christian emblems. A coin of Constantine (317–324) w...
found on the Wall (1909), with the London mint mark PLN a...
bearing two Victories placing on an altar a shield VOT·PR, on t...
face of the altar a cross within a wreath. Two others have th...
cross, a Constantine II and a Crispus, son of Constantine I and ...
Caesar in the West. This inscription means official recogniti...
of Christianity, a solemn affirmation by Constantine of his Christi...
faith.

Towards the end of the Roman occupation it seems that Chris...
anity and Paganism were in free and open competition: at S...
chester the Christian church did not oust the temple of Ma...
At York, says Gordon Home, there is a remarkable dearth ...
Christian edifices in Eburacum, and indeed the whole of Yorkshi...

Temples. Almost every town or station had its temple or templ...
to different deities. It is conjectured that that of Sulis Minerva ...
Bath had a façade *c.* 25 ft. wide, with Corinthian columns, scul...
tured cornice and tall pediment. On the tympanum was a Gorgon ...
head, moustached and bearded. We have noted that there was ...
temple of Neptune and Minerva at Chichester. At Silchester tw...
(of four) temples inside the east gate were in a walled enclosur...
one 73 ft., the other 50 ft. square, either enclosing a square *ce...*
(chamber) raised on a *podium* (platform). A third was sixtee...
sided, 65 ft. diameter, with a *cella* of similar shape. A temple ...
Weycock, near Waltham St. Lawrence (Berks), and its *cella* we...
octagonal: at West Mersea (Essex) was a circular one, 65 ...
diameter, like the temple of Vesta down by the Tiber at Rom...
Most of the temples in Britain, however, were rectangular. Th...
at Caerwent, 45 ft. × 42 ft., had a square *cella* with apse at nor...
end and entrance south; a walled approach led up to it. ...
Lydney the temple of Nodens (Brit. Nudd or Lludd) had rich mosaic...
Measuring 88 ft. × 62 ft., it had a south entrance, and two chape...
on either side accommodated by recesses in the exterior wal...
The oblong *cella* had three compartments along the north wa...
Outside the south-east corner was the verger's room. Voti...

tablets found show that pilgrims came to the shrine to be cured of diseases. The Mithraeum at Housesteads (Borcovicium), already mentioned, was excavated in the side of a hill at a point where a spring issues. The middle part was *c.* 30 ft. × 16 ft. There was a nave between two narrow aisles raised 2 ft. high, where votaries kneeled turned towards the nave. Near the west end a tank received the spring water. There was an inner sanctuary with sculptures. We know also of temples to Jupiter, Mars, Apollo, Serapis, Roma and others.

A form of temple much in use in Britain is that called Roman–Celtic or Gallo-Roman: we have already seen examples at Silchester, Caerwent and Lydney. Generally the structure is a *cella* of about 20 ft. square internally, with walls *c.* 3 ft. thick, set inside a portico measuring about 50 ft. internally. *Cella* and portico were mostly raised *c.* 3 ft. above the level, and approached by a flight of steps. The temple again was set in an enclosure of about 100 ft. square, bounded sometimes by a wall or earth bank or ditch. Such temples were usually built in open country places and on hill-tops, rather than in towns. Dr. Wheeler has described such a temple found on a little hill near Harlow, Essex, and recently another was found close to a Roman road at Titsey (Surrey). In the *cella* the floor would be tessellated, and on a low platform at the back would be an altar or statue; or the cult-object would stand on a base in the centre of the floor. The dedication would be to a Celtic god half Romanized, perhaps identified with Mercury, Apollo, or Mars or some other Roman deity. The origin of the type is a native environment in the Celtic regions north of Provence and west of the Rhine, especially in the Seine and Moselle valleys. Britain has contributed, to date, some fourteen sites, in two of which (Richborough and Colchester) two such temples stood close together. The larger one, at Colchester (south-east of Sheepen Farm), had a *cella* 40 ft. square, walls 4 ft. thick and a veranda wall 64 ft. square: the enclosure was over 400 ft. × 300 ft. This temple was in use for three centuries. Other sites are at Worth (Kent), Lancing and Chanctonbury Ring (Sussex), Harlow and Great Chesterford (Essex), Silchester (Hants), with three examples, Lydney (Glos.), Caerwent (Mon.), Verulamium (Herts), Farley Heath and Titsey (Surrey) and Maiden Castle (Dorset), all in the south and south-east counties from Monmouthshire to Essex. In France some forty examples have been found, and thirteen in Germany, especially round Rouen and Trier (Wheeler, *Antiq. Journal*).

Shrines there were both private and public. In a private house, in dining-room or kitchen, there would be a shrine in honour of the Lares, guardians of the household, the Penates, protectors of household stores, and the Genius or Guardian Spirit of the master of the house, and perhaps another to Venus or some other Graeco-Roman deity. The figure of the deity was put in a small niche, and below it, for offerings, was an altar on which were painted two serpents symbolizing master and mistress. We find small bronze and terracotta figures. A nymphaeum in the garden at the Ched-worth villa was rectangular, 25 ft. × 19 ft., with open front and an apse projecting at the back. Into an octagonal basin sunk in

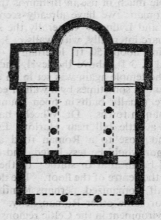

Fig. 15.—Plan of Christian Church at Silchester.

the middle of the floor plashed the water of a spring. Public shrines are those of Street (Lares Compitales) and City deities (Lares Praesides). At the side of a street would be a small room open in front, and sometimes apsidal at back, containing a figure and an altar. Caerwent and Silchester, it is thought, provided examples. The small Christian church at Silchester, measuring 42 ft. × 27 ft., was typical of an early Christian basilica. It was oriented with chancel at the west, and an internal porch at the east end. There was a nave, and two aisles divided by arcades, while at the west end were two transepts screened off from the aisles.

Altars in Britain are all quite Roman in character; they came in and went out with the Romans. They are rectangular blocks of stone, more high than wide, projecting at both base and head, and usually placed against a wall. In the upper surface was generally carved a cavity for libations. Scrolls at the top of the sides are not uncommon, and the sides are often ornamented, while the front panel is reserved for the inscription.

We pass on to cremation and inhumation, tombstones and their inscriptions. Burials both after cremation and by inhumation obtained in Roman Britain, but for the earlier part of the occupation burnt burials prevail. In the open country the discovery of burials generally implies a Roman villa near at hand. There is mostly a cemetery outside the walls of a town, but often the burials are strung out along both sides of a road outside the town gates. At Colchester burials were along the road outside the west gate; and at Verulam and Wroxeter by Watling Street. At Verulam the cemetery recently examined was divided into two parts by a ridgeway (King Harry Lane) running north-west towards Prae Wood. Cremations began c. 80 and continued till c. 160; inhumations were of the 3rd and 4th centuries. Three rectangular, brick-lined burning-chambers were found. Watling Street in Kent and Surrey provides the most notable example, for there is hardly a mile between Blackheath and Canterbury where burials have not been recorded—e.g., at Blackheath, Crayford, Dartford, Southfleet, Strood, Rainham, Newington, Sittingbourne, Bapchild and Faversham. Burials both burnt and unburnt were all along the line of the Roman road from Kingsholm to Wotton (Glos.). Cemeteries have been found outside Bath, at Baldock (Herts), at Welwyn (Herts), Ospringe (Kent), North Ockenden (Essex), Hassocks (Sussex), Eye (Suffolk), and elsewhere. Those at Colchester, Ospringe and Baldock are perhaps the most important.

At Baldock (Walls Field) no fewer than 320 burial groups of from two to thirteen associated objects were found, " together with objects representing at least one hundred other groups, which, owing to inhumations being resorted to at a later period, smashed beyond recall these other unassociated objects " (P. Westell). As a rule the cremated remains at Baldock occupied about one-half to one-third of the containing vessel. Earth only covered the objects. The largest group consists of thirteen objects, one of the largest so far recorded from Britain. In one instance a Samian-ware bowl (form 37) was part of a woman's burial; it contained forty-four beads of pinkish glass, gilded, forming part of a necklace. A typical group (No. 102) of date c. A.D. 150, of seven objects contains, exceptionally, three glass decanters, with reeded handles, the smallest with two, the tallest being 12 in. high and having a moulded circle on the base with the letters M.A.P.—probably the initials of the maker. The very small cinerary urn is only 7½ in. high, and of light buff ware. One object, a saucer, is purposely broken (as usual) so that its spirit might be released with that of the departed: this recalls the breaking of stone axes for Stone-Age burials. In one case with an unburnt burial a coin of Domitian (81–96), Charon's ferry fee, was found in the mouth of a skeleton. Among other relics was a bronze enamelled toilet set consisting of an ear-pick and a nail-cleaner; the appropriate tweezers were missing. The whole of the objects found are in Letchworth Museum (*Soc. Antiq. Scot.*, vol. LXVI). This cemetery, strongly suggesting the near neighbourhood of a Roman-British township, is one of the many indications of Roman settlement of the north and north-east of Herts, more especially along the line of the partly Romanized Icknield Way.

Ospringe is on Watling Street, 10 miles from Canterbury and 16 miles from Rochester, and near it was probably the station of Durolevum. This might account for the large cemetery on both sides of the road, the south side in Syndale Park, found, excavated and reported by Mr. W. Whiting (*Arch. Cant.*, vol. XXXVIII). There were here more burnt than unburnt burials, mainly of early 2nd century, but there was no evidence of sequence in time. Specimens of urns, etc., are seen in the museum on the south side of the road. In one case two bone dice and a set of twenty-four coloured counters were found in an urn beneath the burnt bones. At Eye there were 150 burnt burials in urns in *c.* 120 square yards. Over the bones in the urns was placed fine sand, and over the whole had been put a continuous layer of pebbles to form a kind of paving. The cemetery was rather less than a mile from a " villa ". At the south west angle of the cross-roads at Hassocks (Sussex) was a large Roman–British cemetery dating *c.* 70–250 (see full account in *Sx. A.C.* LXVI, 34 foll.). Such cemetery graves are flat, and the burials shallow, 1½–2 ft. deep.

Separate tumuli or mounds of earth mark the burials of distinguished people. Seven remarkable conical tumuli are the " Bartlow Hills " in Essex, six of which were excavated between 1832 and 1840, and were found to contain a wealth of grave goods. The largest had a diameter of 147 ft., and height of 47 ft. In it was a wooden chest measuring 4½ in. × 3⅛ in. × 2 ft high, and containing for urn a handled glass jar, a bronze jug lying in a bronze saucer, a bronze lamp, two bronze strigils (for scraping the skin after a bath), a folding iron seat, a glass flask, etc. (*Archaeologia*, XXVI). There were two tumuli at Thornborough, Bucks, near the Fescote Villa; one, 40 ft. across and 20 ft. high, was found (1840) to contain a burnt burial, with sword-hilt, a figure of Cupid, vases and a bronze lamp. Again near a villa—250 yds. north-west of it—were the four tumuli at Rougham, near Bury St. Edmunds. The northernmost, called Eastlow Hill, was 100 ft. diameter and 12 ft. high. It was found (1844) to contain, east of its centre, a small vaulted building on a concrete foundation, with walls of flint and tiles *c.* 2 ft. high. The interior measurements of this vault were 7½ ft. × 4½ ft., and it had an arch and gable roof of tiles, stones and mortar. To this tomb at its north end a small projecting chamber *c.* 18 in. square had been added, and contained glass vessels. In the vault itself was a leaden coffin (6 ft. 9 in. × 1 ft. 5 in. × 1 ft. 4 in.) in a wooden shell, enclosing the skeleton of a man over 6 ft. tall, with a corroded coin in his mouth. The tomb furniture in this and the other mounds

FIG. 16.—Tomb with various Grave Furniture, from Avisford, Sussex, 1817.

(for burnt burials) resembled that of the Bartlow Hills—glass urns, iron lamp, iron rods for suspending it, etc.

In some of the cemeteries were located the *ustrina* (burning-floors) on which the bodies were burnt—*e.g.*, at Hassocks (Sussex), Litlington near Royston (Herts.), and Preston near Weymouth. Jars for a handful of the ashes or a few fragments of burnt bones were mostly jars in ordinary domestic use, and were sometimes covered with a lid, stone or tile when put into a hole in the ground: if a covering were desired, it was often contrived with four tiles forming a box and one for the top.

A burnt burial with its grave furniture may be accommodated in a stone chest. All the items were neatly arranged in a sandstone cist in the burial of a person of means at Avisford, near Arundel (Sussex). In both corners at either end had been a small rounded bracket hollowed out of the block and holding a small terracotta lamp. In the centre was a large one-handled bottle of thick, greenish glass, filled with burnt bones. Round it was a remarkable group of vessels of a coarse light-red ware—*e.g.*, three small one-handled jugs, two basins placed in saucers, nine cups of various sizes, two candlesticks with nozzles, and a round one-handled saucer in which was a smooth, oval, white pebble, like a pigeon's egg. In another saucer was a round black stone, and another contained an oyster-shell. At one end were the soles of a pair of small shoes studded with hexagonal-headed bronze nails. A somewhat similar burial was found at Great Coggeshall (Essex).

The change to unburnt or inhumation burials was made in Britain by *c.* 250. In the Isle of Portland (*c.* 1850) were found 200 unburnt burials; 300 were found near Irchester, Northants. Tomb houses were rectangular or circular (as at Lockham, near Maidstone). At Holwood Hill, near Keston (Kent), was a rectangular tomb containing a stone sarcophagus, and two other coffins let into graves; and a circular one as well. Other circular and vaulted tombs were at Chedworth (Glos.) and near Pulborough (Sussex). We have had examples of coins placed in the mouth, but on the whole this practice was rare in this country. The general position of bodies in graves was east to west, the head mostly west. Coffins are of many types—wooden, hewn out of a block of sandstone, limestone or marble, lead decorated with straight lines, zigzags, S-shaped curves and scallops in relief: see in London, York and Colchester museums. The lead coffins are sometimes found in wooden shells: one was so enclosed and deposited in a vault at Upper Slaughter (Glos.). The coffin was often filled with lime. Lastly, here is an example of rough-and-ready burials in country places. At the Hambledon Villa (Chap. V), in a deep pit, were found the bodies of two men, one woman and two young children, hastily thrown in at the end of the 2nd century. The courtyard was "littered" with hastily-buried bodies of babies, mostly new-born, some on top of others. It seems that unwanted children were so disposed of.

Tombstones were stone slabs inscribed in front with epitaphs, often with tops shaped to slope with the pediments. Common is a round-headed niche with figure standing in it: *e.g.*, the Colchester centurion of the XXth, Marcus Favonius, with the staff of office in right hand, and left hand on sword-hilt (Plates, p. vi). Sometimes there is more than one figure. Examples of epitaphs: Cirencester: Rufus Sita eques coh VI Tracum ann. LX Stip. XXII heredes ex test. curavere h:s.f. (Rufus Sita cavalryman of the 6th cohort of Thracians, 60 years of age, 22 years of service: his heirs in accordance with his will had this erected). He is laid here. Silchester: Memoriae Fl. Victorinae T. Tam. Victor coniunx posuit. (In memory. To Flavia V. her husband Victor placed this.)

CHAPTER IX

ARTS AND CRAFTS

ROMAN art flourished in Britain, more especially in the lowland zone. Enough remains have been discovered to serve as samples of the kind of art and handicraft that was familiar to the Roman–Briton during nearly the whole of the occupation. In the bigger towns—e.g., Londinium and Corinium—were to be seen in plenty by the ordinary man samples of architectural art, statues in public places, statuettes in temples and in his home, mosaic and plain tessellated pavements, frescoed walls, leadwork, pewter-work, pottery and glass vessels, bronze brooches, bracelets, necklaces, beads and so on. A citizen of Londinium could complain of no lack of the products of Roman art: there " art entered everywhere, modestly, but with confidence and tenacity ": the diffusion of art was probably greater than among Londoners of the 20th century. The majority of artistic things, it is true, were executed on the Continent, but some few were undoubtedly of native make.

Art, however, though plentiful, was of the Roman imperial brand, not of a high order, maintaining little more than a dull level of imitation. " The artistic romanization of Britain is a melancholy story " (Collingwood). The skill of the pre-Roman Celt in inventing abstract designs in curved lines vanished, or went into close retirement, soon after the Roman conquest, and there stayed till the departure of the eagles early in the 5th century. Artistically, the Roman conquest was a disastrous change.

The works of artist and handicraftsman to be described in this chapter are divisible into four classes: works of art (e.g., sculpture) in Roman style (a) imported into and used in Britain, (b) made in Britain by Roman hands, (c) made here by British hands under Roman instruction and (d) in Celtic style made by Britons themselves. It would be hard to determine which (e.g.) mosaic pavements or painted walls belong to (b) or (c), as no doubt Romans taught Britons to decorate floors, to paint wall-plaster and to carve stone. Very few items can be assigned to (d): even the famous Gorgon's head of Bath is not certainly one of them.

Architectural carvings in stone, often of considerable merit, figured in the public buildings of towns. Thus at Cirencester there was handsome work in pillar-shafts, cornices, moulded friezes, and Roman Corinthian capitals with two tiers of acanthus leaves. A Corinthian capital excavated in 1808 was 4 ft. across, implying a

117

column at least 30 ft. high. Four figures of very good work, representing a Bearded Bacchus, Silenus, Youthful Bacchus and a Bacchante, start from the acanthus leaves so as to appear to support the abacus. There was also an Attic column base with two tori of the same diameter; and a carved head of Jupiter used as the keystone of an arch. Here was, then, a building of some architectural pretensions. On the temple of Sulis Minerva at Bath was a sculptured pediment and ornamental frieze in good Roman style. The forum and basilica of London are the only big public buildings found (1881) in the capital. The basilica, measuring 233 ft. × 58 ft., had an apse at either end, and two ranges of Corinthian columns to separate nave and aisles; some of the capitals are in Reading Museum. Further, there were Corinthian columns in the basilicas at Wroxeter and Caerwent, in the latter case the shafts 3 ft. diameter, being decorated with leaf pattern. It can hardly be doubted that statues of emperors rose in a central position in the fora of towns, and in the basilicas statues with mural crowns symbolizing the genius of the town. London, Silchester and Cirencester would not in this respect be behind Continental towns like Nemausus (Nîmes). The Genius of a castrum was found at Netherby (the Wall), wearing a mural crown, holding a horn of plenty and pouring a libation on to an altar as offering to the superior powers. Britain itself was probably personified in statues, the figure derived from a seated Roma: such a figure was revived for the English coinage in 1685. Of river gods there were statues of Father Thames (torso in London Museum), and of the North Tyne, a figure reclining on the left arm, with long, curling hair and beard. Large parts of figures of Hercules, Apollo and Minerva Custos chiselled out of " Barnack rag " (oolite) were found near Wansford (Beds.) in 1884–1886, and are now in the collection of the Duke of Bedford. A stone figure of Atys, shepherd-priest of Cybele, was found in the City of London. He wears Phrygian cap, tunic and cloak fastened by a brooch on the right shoulder; a bow is held in his left hand (*B.M. Guide*, 27). Smaller statuary of good quality is found on tombs: thus in Guildhall Museum is a portrait of a signifer (standard-bearer) in relief, probably dating from the early 2nd century, which Lethaby describes as " a masterly work of unflattered portraiture ". The well-known Colchester Centurion, Favonius Facilis (Plate VI), is also fine work.

On the exterior of private buildings there was very little architectural art, but interiors showed decorations of a certain standard of excellence. Chief among these were tessellated and mosaic pavements. In Chap. V reference was made to those at Wood-

hester and Bignor. For splendid illustrations of pavements
. Lysons' *Reliquiae Britannico-Romanae*, Morgan's *Romano-
British Mosaics*, and a shorter account in Ward's *Romano-British
Buildings*, Chap. XII, should be consulted. Here is attempted a
brief account of the style of decoration, construction and materials
of such pavements. Of the several pavements found at Cirencester,
the subjects of one or two will be described. One is concerned with
marine subjects: Neptune in his chariot, Cupid on a dolphin, marine
dragons, a sea leopard and a sea horse, several kinds of fish,
specially the conger eel, lobsters, crabs, starfish and shells: all
these, from the natural history point of view, accurately done.
In the famous pavement of the Barton, in the centre of the circle
is staged Orpheus playing on his lyre, while around him are birds—
duck, goose, hen-peacock, pheasants, etc.—which are separated
by a wreath of bay-leaves (three deep) from wild animals—lion,
panther, leopard and tiger pacing with dignified restraint to the
music, as at Woodchester, where the pavement is probably by
the same artist. The drawing of the beasts compels admiration.
They are set out " with an ease and mastery that is remarkable.
There is grace in their gesture that has seldom been reached in the
art of even the highest period of the life of a nation." Such is the
opinion of Mr. A. Powell, who repaired the pavement. The
pavement from Dyer Street had four female figures symbolizing
the four seasons—a common theme—and, of these, medallions
of Flora, Ceres and Pomona remain. Flora, representing Spring,
is a head and shoulders in a circle, with a chaplet of ruby-coloured
and white flowers set off among leaves, extending over the crown
and sides of the face. A shapely bird is perched on the left shoulder,
while against the right rests a flowering branch. The ruby flowers
are composed of tessellae of glass. The brighter-coloured tessellae
are of coloured glass also in the Bacchus Mosaic (British Museum)
found in 1803 under the East India House, Leadenhall Street. The
pattern of this is 11 ft. square, and was laid in a floor at least 22 ft.
square. Bacchus is riding " side-saddle " on a fierce tiger.

All such pictures are set off by borders with contrasting colours:
as a rule the decorated panel has a monochrome margin, rather like
a carpet of today with its surround of polished boards or linoleum.
Skilfully used, such borders add much to the effect of the whole.
Among the common borders are the guilloch, a loose cable
of two or three plaited strands; the cresting wave, the crests
exaggerated into spirals; the fret (key) or labyrinth; and large
triangles arranged apex to base. Perhaps the most attractive
borders are series of scrolls with foliage. On the big pavement

at Woodchester is an elaborate border. "Its outermost borde
was a red stripe; then followed in succession key pattern of shade
red on a dark ground, a wide labyrinth in black on a white groun
a narrow braid of shaded red on a dark ground, and an extreme
wide member formed of square compartments filled with elabora
geometrical ornamentations, and last an innermost or secon
guilloch" (Ward). This wide member consisted of sixteen rec
angular panels containing geometrical ornaments, and eight circle

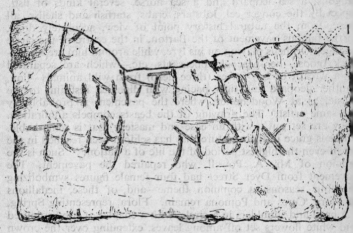

FIG. 17.—A Graffito on a Pila Tile from Wiggonholt, Sussex, in full:

Pilares (Pillar Tiles): Number not Stated.
Cuni(e) ati lateres (Wedge-shaped Hollow Voussoirs): 4.
Tubuli (Flue Tiles) Numeravi 500: I have counted 500.

A Tile-maker's Note of Output.

near, but not at, the corners. In the centre of the circles we
alternately, vases and star-flowers. The mosaic-workers too
special pains with the ornaments—geometrical, convention
flowers, mythological groups, etc.—of the compartments a
medallions. The main divisions of the decorative scheme we
rectilinear or curvilinear, or a combination of both. Thus a circ
is included in a square, leaving four spandrels in the angles, whi
are filled in with figures, chalices, heart-shaped leaves, etc.
circle may be divided into compartments by bands radiati
from a small inner circle. A pavement at Horkstow, Barton-o
Humber, had three compartments. To the west was a circ

diameter $18\frac{1}{2}$ ft., containing Orpheus with beasts and birds; in
the centre a circle, diameter $15\frac{5}{8}$ ft., with radii, as above; and at the
east end a chariot race, in which four bigae are competing, one
having just come to grief by the loss of a wheel. A recently found
(1930–1931) panel at Verulamium represents Ocean or Neptune,
similar to panels at Withington and Frampton, set in a fret border,
which had an eight-leaved flower at each corner, and a two-handled
vase in the middle of each side. In the centre is the figure: shoulders
and head, bearded and moustached, with horns coming from the
top of the forehead. There is a guilloch border at the bottom.

To pass from decoration to construction. Such pavements were
laid on a floor a foot or more thick, made up of two or three coats
of coarse, strong mortar. The floor rested on pillars $2\frac{1}{2}$–$3\frac{1}{2}$ ft.
high, mostly built with tiles 8 in. square and $c.$ $1\frac{3}{4}$ in. thick. Bigger
tiles, sometimes 11 in. square, were used for the base of the pillars
and for the capitals on which the floor rested directly. Thus at
Cirencester the measurements were: tesserae set in fine mortar,
? in.; a layer of pounded brick, lime and sand, $4\frac{1}{2}$ in.; a layer of
gravel, lime, sand, broken tiles and rubble, 6 in.; rammed gravel,
? in.; total thickness, 14 in. Box-shaped flue tiles, open at the
bottom to admit the heat generated in the hypocaust, were ranged
one over the other vertically up the side walls, so as to form continuous pipes running up the walls of the room above and discharging the gases under the eaves. Third, the materials of the
tessellae at Cirencester were as follows. Natural: white, hard
chalk—cream, freestone from the Great Oolite—grey, the same
heated—yellow, oolite—chocolate, Old Red Sandstone—slate or
black, limestone of the Lower Lias. Artificial: light red, dark
red and black, terracotta—ruby, glass.

Somerset and Gloucestershire are rich in figured pavements,
and three others may be mentioned besides those already described:
Littlecote (Wilts), Bramdean (Hants), and Brading (I.o.W.).

Interior walls were very often painted, exterior walls also sometimes. The ground on which the colours were laid was a plaster
or finely sifted gravel, lime and sand, in roughly equal proportions,
about $\frac{3}{4}$ in. thick. On this was laid very evenly the stucco, or face
plaster, the " skimming coat ", of finely prepared lime (sometimes
of powdered shells), very thin. While this coat was still damp the
mass of the colour was laid on with a trowel, by the process called
" fresco ". The colours were mixed with size as a fixing agent.
Panels were thus laid vertically up the wall, in blue, dark or Pompeian red, green, orange and purple, separated by lines of black.
Then with a brush were put in ornaments of waved lines, circles,

etc., and figures, mythological and other. Inscriptions were introduced in a colour contrasting with the background. Pieces of fresco can be seen at the British, Guildhall and London Museums and at the Society of Antiquaries, Burlington House. From these and similar fragments we can gather some facts. Pilasters of about 8 in. wide might be adorned with foliage branching from a vertical stem, or might be simply vertical strips in plain colour. Dadoes in black were common, with wreaths, festoons and birds. In the panels was a great variety of small ornaments: little scenes in circles—e.g., two young lovers, cupids floating in air, winged horses, Silenus heads, tigers, bears, dogs, metal cups, all proportionately very small. Dancing figures in Pompeian manner often occupied the panels; and imitation of marble was much in evidence (see Rochester Museum). The results were pleasing; and we should remember that they were generally produced by "the ordinary journeyman decorator's work of the time". Marble linings of Purbeck and porphyry were also employed for walls, especially for dadoes, and fragments of them have been found at Woodchester, Silchester, Colchester, Folkestone and elsewhere.

Statues and Statuettes of Bronze.—Many dozens of bronze statuettes survive: Jupiter, Hercules, Apollo, Atys, Mars, Mercury with winged head, wand and purse, Diana with bow and quiver; many of these are good. There was evidently in London a big bronze statue of Hadrian, the head of which was found in the Thames (1834), possibly a memorial of his visit to Britain in 121, though he is represented as several years younger than at that date (Plate I). He has a close-clipped beard and moustache, and a double row of curly locks of hair from ear to ear; the mouth is strong. Perhaps the best bronze statuette is that (found at Barking Hall, Suffolk) of the Emperor Nero in Roman costume and armour, 22 in. high, probably a Gaulish work; but a good second is the figure of an archer from Cheapside, London.

It is impossible in small space to describe one tenth of the various forms of pottery ware in use. Much was imported from Gaul, from the Rhineland and elsewhere; but probably the greater part of such wares was made in Britain, often on Continental models. On the whole, except in wealthy homes, the assemblage of pottery on a table must have made a drab show. The so-called "coarse" wares were black, brown and grey, the black sometimes burnished; a few brown pots relieved the general monotony with a mica-dusted surface. A buff-coloured basin (*mortarium*) with flanged edges and specially gritted bottom was much in use as a kitchen utensil for pounding food, as was also the tall wine-jar (*amphora*

th two handles. Imported in vast quantities, especially to
ondon c. 60–85, were the " Samian " or terra sigillata vessels of
ral or sealing-wax red, ornamented in relief with scrolls, figures
men and animals in panels, saltire crosses and conventional
owers of many kinds. Of these there was a very great variety,
rtainly no fewer than a hundred shapes, of which between a dozen
d twenty were almost universal. The names of the makers are
nerally stamped on the inside of the base or among the ornaments
the outside—e.g., Vitalis, Saturnus, Rufinus, Aestivus. These
it a little of the joy of colour into a meal. A study of this very
teresting subject may be made with Oswald and Pryce's *Intro-
ction to the Study of Terra Sigillata*; but a small selection of the
mmonest forms, among which are Nos. 18, 27, 29, 30, 33 and 37,
illustrated and described in *B.M. Guide*, p. 106 onwards. Moulds
r the production in Britain of Samian vessels have been found at
olchester and Pulborough. The red of the paste was produced
the use of peroxide of iron, and of the glaze with ferrous sulphate.
mewhat more fragile, but more interesting in their designs, were
e slate-coloured vessels of " Castor " ware, decorated in raised
eamy slip with hunting scenes—dogs chasing hares, stags or wild
ars—and with flowing decoration of curved tendrils reminiscent
the Celtic art which the Roman conquest almost suppressed,
it which contrived to keep alive in the background and reassert
elf after 410. Many Castor forms differ from those of coarse
d Samian wares. In the New Forest were made pots of a hard
ey stoneware, with a purple glaze on the exterior. In other
ssels—e.g., saucers and bowls—we have a soft, buff-coloured
ound adorned with circles and wavy stripes of thin, brick-red
lour, laid on before firing with a liquid ferruginous paint. New
orest manufacture lasted till the end of the Roman period.
Numerous Roman–British pottery kilns have been discovered—
;., at Colchester, London, Farnham, and in the New Forest
lants), Somersetshire, Dorsetshire, Staffordshire, and at Upchurch
ent). The majority of them are small and circular, the baking-
or, perforated with holes, raised on a centre post like a single-
gged table; into the lower chamber was pushed the fuel through a
aight passage, the stoke-hole being outside. The plan is like a
w's harp. A dome of clay was made freshly for each firing.
pottery manufactory might comprise a dozen or twenty of such
ns separated by only a few yards: a kiln from such a group at
attisfield (Suffolk) was recently moved bodily to the Ipswich
useum. When the site was being prepared for St. Paul's Cathedral
e remains of many potters' kilns were found, and also, but far

fewer, of glass furnaces. The great majority of glass vessels use
in Britain, and those of the best quality, were imported fro
Syria, Italy, Belgium and Cologne, but glass was certainly ma
here, especially for windows. This was thickish, and of a light gre
or blue tint. It is recognized by the fact that on one side it
polished, on the other rough. The metal was poured into a shallo
stone mould, which left its mark on the rough side. Glass cu
with moulded reliefs of chariot races or gladiatorial comba
(c. A.D. 100), with the names of the competitors above, are in t
British and Colchester Museums; one such was found at t
Roman Villa at Hartlip (Kent). A characteristic Roman glass bo
is ornamented with strips applied from base to lip—'' pillar glass
Small bottles for unguents and perfumes were 3–6 in. long, an
$\frac{3}{4}$–$1\frac{1}{2}$ in. diameter. The Maidstone Museum has a good collectio
of Roman glassware, but the best place for a study of it is probab
the King Edward VII gallery of the British Museum.

Silver was extracted from British lead and refined—e.g., at S
chester, Wroxeter, and Hengistbury Head (Hants)—and made i
into many forms more or less artistic, such as the votive inscriptio
from Barkway (Herts), with small figures of Vulcan and Mars t
Avenger. There were silver bracelets, bowls, dishes and finge
rings. In the important hoard of silver found (1854) near Colerai
Co. Derry, Ireland, were two axe-shaped ingots, one stamp
Ex Of(ficina) Patrici (from the workshop of Patricius), and
neatly ornamented hemispherical bowl, the designs being punch
in dots and circles from the outside. Fragments of silver pla
are in geometrical style—e.g., in one case guilloch separati
panels of diaper pattern, and in another interlocked triangl
within a foliated circle. Several hoards of silver have been found
e.g., at Traprain Law and at Corbridge. From the latter is a la
(dish) of careful and good workmanship, in the possession of t
Duke of Northumberland. This flat, slightly hollow dish, measu
ing 19 in. × 15 in. and weighing 148 oz. troy, is supported on a r
or foot 1 in. high. The ornament was first cast in a mould, th
chased, and the spaces between the ornaments engraved with t
burin. The details are Greek rather than Roman, and the pie
may have come from Ephesus; its date is c. 300. The subject i
late version of the Judgement of Paris, and we have Apollo f
Paris, and Delphi for Mount Ida. From right to left the figu
are: Apollo standing in a shrine, with his gryphon below, He
seated, Aphrodite, Athena and Artemis, with her dog and a dyi
stag below.

Gold jewellery may be illustrated by specimens found in a hoa

Llandovery (Carmarthenshire). A long gold chain with eight-
ped links had attached to it a wheel pendant of eight spokes,
a crescent; the chain was worn double round the neck, wheel
back and crescent in front, the amulets being associated with the
ship of sun and moon. There were also two small gold bracelets
resenting snakes: one has green glass eyes and tapers to the tail.
ilar snake-bracelets come from Newport Pagnell (Bucks)
Southfleet (Kent). An elaborate gold brooch was found
Odiham (Hants). Gold finger-rings, sometimes massive, are
ly common—e.g., with angular shoulders in open work from
ester (Som.), dated to the middle of the 3rd century by a coin of
erus Alexander (222–235) set in the bezel. An ear-ring of gold
e has a slip-knot for adjustment.

efore the advent of the Romans the art of enamelling on metals
been widely and successfully practised. Caskets, bowls and
oches were tastefully ornamented with colours of bright orange,
and blue. During the Roman period enamelling continued,
cially on brooches, and Celtic ornament to some extent survived.
ittle enamelled bowl (B.M.) was found at Braughing (Herts), a
arkable enamelled plate in the shape of an altar was recovered
n the Thames, and an enamelled bronze model stool came from
ury, Surrey. Seal-boxes have enamelled lids. In bronze
oches also Celtic artistry managed to survive, though somewhat
ariously. In the early 2nd century such brooches were being
duced, but nearly all of them in the north, in Brigantia, in Scot-
l, and in Ireland. A very fine example is the well-known gold
la from Aesica (the Wall). The safety-pin brooch shaped like a
is a very old friend, deriving from a millennium before the
nan conquest. Originally made of one piece of wire, it had at
head of the bow a spiral spring, and the point rested in the turned-
dge, made by flattening out and turning up the edge of the wire,
he catch-plate. Gradually a hinge supplanted the coil and
me general. Thus the so-called Aucissa brooch, distributed
n Gaul in the 1st century, and of Celtic origin, was hinged.
issa was one of the makers of this type, and stamped his name
he head: examples have been found in Somerset, at Cirencester,
n Hill (Taunton Museum), and Wroxeter, and two are in Hull
eum. A harp-shaped brooch with an ornamented knot at the
and a collar-moulding round the centre of the bow, as found at
by Thore, Westmorland, is attractive: its date is c. 150. The
ration of scroll work and enamelling shows British influence.
amelled brooches date from the second and third centuries,
are common in Britain and abroad, especially in Belgium "

(*B.M. Guide*). Among these is "the British S or dragones
brooch", mostly from the north; and disc-shaped brooches con
in front to a low cone, with coloured wedges arranged roun
circle in the centre. These are but a few of the very many types

Bronze articles of toilet were numerous. Thus from a crema
burial at Coddenham (Suffolk) comes a circular flat bronze
2½ in. diameter and 2 in. deep. On the outside of the lid w
medallion of an emperor (? Vespasian), and on its underside a s
convex metallic mirror. In bronze also are small lamps and
with handles. An attractive piece of bronze decoration is a sw
scabbard from the Thames, the main part of it a compositio
floral scrolls, with birds, butterflies and rabbits in the spaces.

Leadwork must have been quite common, for Britain du
the whole Roman period was one of the chief sources of this me
Over fifty inscribed pigs of lead have been found in Britain, and th
having been lost in transit, represent a very large output (see C
X). The mining areas were in the Mendips, Shropshire and N
Derbyshire.

In excavating buildings one often finds pieces of sheet lead
had belonged to the more important roofs, and leaden pipes are
uncommon. The bottom of the hot-water bath at Bath was cov
with lead (1864). To lead coffins reference was made above (C
VIII). They are often ornamented with lattice lines in re
with shells in the middle of the squares. In a round lead can
(British Museum) were deposited burnt bones in a glass urn fr
cremation. Lead water cisterns have been found. Bronze
for writing on wax on a tablet, and bronze pens, both with era
at the other end, and bronze spoons were apparently plentifu

Of pewter, many 4th-century ingots of which, stamped with
seal of one Syagrius, were found in the Thames at Battersea,
made a variety of vessels and dishes, especially in the south-
There is no reason why these should not have been native Br
work. The composition is roughly 75 per cent. tin, 25 per cent.

Iron objects are very plentiful, and indeed the Roman tool
was almost as well furnished as a modern one. Two hoard
ironsmith's work were found at Silchester, and another at C
Chesterford, and these, as Ward says, "will give the reade
insight into the ironmongery of the era". For a classified lis
his *Roman Era*, p. 195. There was a great variety of knives,
with ornamented bone grips—*e.g.*, carved with a hound chasi
hare. Iron nave-bands for wheels of vehicles were common
in earlier La Tène times. Of horse-shoes attached by nails, t
with a wavy outline go back to the Roman period. Planes, hamr

atchets, chisels, tongs, drills, pincers, gouges, files, saws and axes
ave been found: a socketed chisel, *c.* 10½ in. long, is in the London
Tuseum.   Locks and keys are of many sorts.   Iron strigils were
ckle-shaped instruments used for scraping the body after the
ath or exercise.   Rings, pins, needles, forks, skewers, spits, hooks,
irgical instruments, styli and lamps are other objects of iron.

There were useful articles in leather and bone: of the former
naterial a great variety of ornamental shoes were made, *e.g.* a shoe
om Southfleet, Kent (*B.M. Guide*, 50), and of the latter pins,
odkins, spoons and a host of other small articles.   To judge
om the frequency with which ornaments of jet and shale occur in
xcavations, there must have been a big trade in them.   Jet came
lostly from the cliffs at Sandsend near Whitby, and shale from
Limmeridge, on the Dorset coast.   Bracelets and pins, and spindle-
horls ornamented with concentric circles and dots, are perhaps
ie commonest articles.   These materials were turned on a lathe.

CHAPTER X

INDUSTRIES, MANUFACTURES, COMMERCE

THE mining of gold, silver, lead and iron and other metals had be
carried on in Britain before the arrival of the Romans. With lea
at any rate, the Romans lost no time, organizing it practically
once when Vespasian's drive westward had secured the Mendi
Mine labour was at first that of slaves, but later free labour w
increased. Roman mining methods in Britain were concerned wi
deposits of ore lying on or close below the surface, seldom wi
the driving of levels or adits. If the veins were thin, they we
followed with trenches, and cut out with pick, hammer and chis
The ore was put into baskets with oak shovels coming to the sha
point of a "spade" in a pack of cards; and the baskets we
shouldered away for sorting and washing. In shallow workir
drainage could be baled out with buckets, and ventilation w
probably not a serious matter. Such galleries as were driv
could be lighted by oil-lamps placed in frequent niches. A valua
pictorial illustration of mining operations and melting was t
fortunately lost when a farmer at Pitney (Somerset) destroyed
fine tessellated pavement. For lead, the furnaces, as at Pen
(Flint), had foundations of solid blocks of stone laid in, and partia
lined with clay, and were used for a series of heats. Coal was us
among other fuels. For silver-refining a cupellation hearth w
used: the lead, melted on a bed of bone-ash, is thus absorb
while the silver is left pure in the shape of pellets. The satura
cupel (bone-ash) was re-smelted for the lead, which was cast i
pigs marked EX ARG(ENTARIIS)—i.e., from the silver-works.

Most of the mines were imperial property, managed by p
curators, who might lease to companies or individuals (conductor
on profitable terms—e.g., by paying a royalty as much as 50 per ce
In Derbyshire pigs are stamped with the names of private perso
It is clear that distribution was well organized: the product of c
lease-holder has been found in Notts, Yorks and Sussex, in the l
case at Broomer's Hill near Pulborough, where four pigs w
found together (one in B.M.), being 23 in. long, 6½ in. wide, a
4¾ in. thick, and weighing 184 lb. The inscription on all four
(TIB.) CL. TR. LVT. BR. EX ARG—i.e., Tiberii Claudii Tr(ophim
Lutudarense Britannicum ex argentariis—British lead from Lu
darum (near Matlock, Derbyshire) belonging to T.C. Tr., from
silver-works (desilvered). These were made in the reign of Domiti

The pigs were found in the top of a bank, and were probably hidden there, not casually dropped. Such pigs were either used as required in Britain, or exported. Losses in transport seem to have been frequent: two pigs from Flint were found in Staffordshire, others near Stockbridge (Hants) and Cheshunt (Herts), and two from the Mendips at Bitterne (Clausentum), the Roman port near Southampton, whence they were probably carried to St. Valéry-sur-Somme.

To consider the minerals more in detail—coal, gold, copper, lead, iron and tin. Coal from the outcrops of our modern coal areas was known to, and used by, the Romans, though they preferred wood fuels. Sometimes they got it by shafts and galleries. In both burnt and unburnt state it has been found in camps on the Wall and in civil sites—*e.g.*, houses at Wroxeter—and (from the Somerset deposits) for the perpetual fires in the temple of Sulis Minerva, Bath. " Coal never became a commercial asset ".

Gold was worked near Dolaucothy (Carmarthen): for the washing process a water channel hewn in rock was brought 7 miles to the spot. A bath-house was provided. A high level of mining skill is revealed here, by the discovery of beams for propping, boards and branches, a shovel-shaped cradle, a corner of a wooden tray, and part of a drainage wheel of 13–14 ft. diameter.

Copper was never extensively produced here by the Romans, but it was mined in Anglesey and North Wales and the centre district of the Welsh borders. There have been found cakes of copper (bun-ingots), roughly circular, diameter *c.* 1 ft., thickness 1–3 in., the result of ladling of the molten metal into a shallow mould (B.M.). The date of the workings is probably *c.* 75–125. Copper smelting was practised in a small way in many places—*e.g.*, Hengistbury Head (Hants) and Silchester.

Lead. From 43 to *c.* 200 lead, plentiful and easily won from the surface, was the most important product of Britain; second only to Spain in this commodity. Export, beginning under Nero (54–68), was very active under Vespasian (69–79), the lead being chiefly worked in five districts—the Mendips, Flintshire, Derbyshire, Yorkshire and Shropshire. Lead was worked, but not desilvered in pre-Roman days. On the Mendips near Charterhouse Farm was a large and civilized mining community, complete with amphitheatre. This was the most important British lead area. The ore was won entirely from surface workings. From inscribed pigs we know that production had begun under Claudius in 49; that under Nero (60) lead was being desilvered. There are five pigs recorded for Vespasian (69–79), three EX ARG., one for Hadrian, three for

Antoninus Pius (one of which weighs 223 lb.—the heaviest found
in Britain—with base 23½ in. by 6¾ in.), and one for Marcus Aurelius.
In brief, there is evidence for Mendip lead-working between 50 and
169. Of the Flintshire works several pigs of Vespasian survive,
two from Chester dating 74, some inscribed DECEANGL, the
tribe Deceangli. Furnaces at Pentre, near Flint, show continuation
of lead-smelting from *c.* 70 to 150. The chief lead-mining area in
Derbyshire was round Matlock, and here the pigs mostly bear private
names, one that of Hadrian (117–138), under whom elsewhere the pro-
curatores took control from private hands. All show the name of a
place in the area, Lutudarum. In Yorkshire two pigs from Nid-
derdale (date 81) have a side inscription BRIG—*i.e.,* the Brigantes.
The Shropshire industry was round Shelve and Minsterly, the
pigs all inscribed Hadrian: one was from near Bishop's Castle.
Almost all Roman lead was desilverized: EX ARG = Ex argentariis, from the silver-works. (On this subject consult Prof. Gowland, *Archaeologia,* LVII, 402.)

Of *iron* Britain was never an important source of supply; as
Caesar said, *eius exigua est copia,* and it is not certain whether it
was officially controlled. In camps on the Wall it was smelted,
e.g., at Corbridge, and at Wilderspool and Richborough. The two
great districts for the industry were the Sussex Weald, where there
was a long pre-Roman period of production and where iron was
smelted during the whole of the occupation, and the Forest of Dean,
especially at Weston-under-Penyard (Herefordshire), the Roman
Ariconium (Bury Hill, 1 mile north-east of Weston Church), where
the *floruit* was *c.* 250–360. A pre-Roman site was developed at
Lydney (Glos.). The iron was produced direct from the ore, with
charcoal (sometimes coal) as fuel. Iron slag was greatly used for
road construction—*e.g.,* the "Iron Way" and Stane Street, both in
Sussex. In Sussex the stress was in the 2nd century, and the iron
field extended from East Grinstead (the Medway) in the north-west
to Westfield (the Brede) in the south-east—*c.* 30 miles. The
outlets for production were the ports at Pevensey and West Hythe,
and the Ouse mouth near Seaford. The north-west region near
East Grinstead could transport to the Thames by the "Iron Way"
(Chap. III) (*Wealden Iron,* by Ernest Straker and *V. C. H. Sussex*
III, 29–32). Some iron was got in other places—*e.g.,* Warwick-
shire, Northamptonshire, Rutland, Lincolnshire, Nottinghamshire,
Cheshire and Northumberland. The smelting was done in a bowl
furnace—*i.e.,* a hole in the ground lined with clay: the blast was
introduced over the edge of the bowl. Iron goods were made
everywhere, in villa and town. There was a forge in the villa at
Folkestone, and another at Colliton Park, Dorchester.

Tin. The Romans had little to do with Britain west of Exeter, until the pre-Roman tin industry was re-established in Cornwall . 250 onwards. A wedge-shaped block of tin of the period, 21 in. long and weighing some 40 lb., is in Truro Museum. Datable objects of tin and pewter belong to the 3rd and 4th centuries. A fine set of pewter dishes was found at Appleshaw, Hants (B.M.). Gowland states that Roman pewter usually contained 71·5 per cent. tin and 27·8 per cent. lead (further see G. Clement Whittick on " Roman Mining in Britain," *Trans. Newcomen Society*, XII).

Of manufactures, pottery and glass-making were mentioned in Chap. IX.

Bricks and tiles were essentially a Roman introduction. The legions, the *Classis Britannica*, the auxiliary troops had their tile-works; so had some of the towns; and there were obviously also private concerns, working near a road for ease in transport. The great tilery of the XXth at Holt, Cheshire, was dug out recently: tiles, cylindrical drain-pipes, flue-tiles, etc., were found in great quantities, marked with the stamp of the legion, as were also burnt-clay antefixes used as ornaments at the edge of roofs. The *Classis Britannica* stamped its tiles CL.BR., as at Folkestone, Dover and Hythe. A furnace of the more private kind was dug out a few years ago at Ewhurst, Surrey; and several others are known up and down the country—*e.g.*, at Stanstead Park (Rowlands Castle), Woolmer, Crondall, Bentley, Bramdean and Basingstoke; all these, with others, in Hants. The workers seem to have enjoyed marking the damp clay with words. Such graffiti have often been found. Textiles were, as they still are in many districts, a domestic industry. Wherever a Roman house is discovered, there will be spindle-whorls and loom-weights of baked clay or stone. A British warm cloak—the mosaic *Winter* at Bignor is dressed in one—was well known commercially, and produced at an imperial weaving-mill at Venta (Winchester). Fulling and dyeing were practised in special wings of villas, as at Chedworth, Darenth (Kent) and Titsey (Surrey).

For *agriculture*, wheat, cattle and hides were exported in pre-Roman times, but it seems doubtful whether the export of wheat could have continued after the conquest. The growth of population and the presence of many thousands of troops whose needs had to be supplied by an *annona* (forced contribution) must have made it difficult for Britain to grow enough wheat for itself. When certain ancient authors quote the case of Britain's supplying wheat to the Rhineland under the Emperor Julian, it was a case of " a special forced levy ", as Collingwood points out: " There was no question of a commercial transaction." The same principle applies when

Constantius Chlorus sent British masons and carpenters to Gau
to rebuild Autun: Gaul had suffered, and the assistance given t
her was by corvée.

On the whole, during the 1st century the balance of trade mus
have been against Britain. The wealthier Britons who though
it in their interest at any cost to worship the great god of Roma
Respectability, were soon purchasers of luxury articles from th
Continent, debtors to foreign traders and under the thumb of foreig
money-lenders. True, by about 150 British home-made product
on Roman lines—*e.g.*, in ironmongery and pottery—were reducin
imports. Still, cattle, iron in small quantities, hunting-dogs an
oysters, brooches from the north for a short time, and fourth
century cloth can hardly have redressed the balance of imports
" Samian " ware and other pottery and glass in enormous quantitie
the best class of metal goods for a century or so, wine and oil fror
Italy and Spain. These and other imported commodities of th
cross-Channel trade kept busy the harbours of London, Southamp
ton Water and the Humber. Some notes on coinage follow in th
next chapter (XI).

CHAPTER XI

COINAGE

BEFORE the conquest Roman coinage had infiltrated to a considerable extent into Britain—*e.g.*, at Colchester—so that during the early stages Roman coins, already familiar (over 150 pre-Claudian coins have been found at Richborough alone during the last fifteen years), were easily accepted as commercially necessary, and the native gold and tin coinage gradually died out. However, the officially issued coinage not proving plentiful enough, it was much imitated; then in the 2nd century Roman coins were so abundant that imitation was no longer necessary. In the 3rd century there was again a shortage, and barbarous copies multiplied exceedingly until there was monetary chaos. In an attempt to amend this, Carausius (Ch. I, K) started a mint at London, and probably others at Bitterne (or Colchester) and Wroxeter. Coins were stamped M.L. —*i.e.*, Moneta Londiniensis. The London mint continued in operation till *c.* 326, and, after an interval, again from 368 till *c.* 393. It is curious that a silver ingot stamped *ex of (ficina) Fl(avii) Honorini*, along with some gold coins, was found (1777) close to the present Mint. The reforms of Diocletian (Ch. I, L) made Government money plentiful again all through the Constantinian epoch: Constantinian coins are by far the most numerous in excavations. Then came the final decline, and for coins Britain had to fend for herself. New Roman copper ceased to reach her. The official coinage from the Continent ends with Honorius (Ch. I, N). The trouble of the early 5th century prevented the arrival of military aid, and therefore of supplies of coins for payment of troops: the Gallic mints ceased to produce bronze. To these late years belong enormous quantities of small (*c.* ½ in. diameter) copper coins called *minimi* which are dug up in late occupation layers. They are barbarous and illegible, imitations of " radiate " coins of Claudius II and Tetricus and of diademed coins of Constantine I and his family.

At Richborough over 55,500 coins (exclusive of post-Roman) have been found in the last forty years, and many thousands before that date. Coins found at this chief port of entry are probably a rough index of comparative intensity of use throughout Britain. Here are some points in the distribution over reigns. Claudius, 51; Flavian, 331; Nerva to Commodus, 456; 3rd century radiates to Numerianus, 7,933; Carausius and Allectus, 1,638; Constantine to Jovian, with Urbs Roma coins, 13,654; House of Valentinian,

133

2,415; House of Theodosius, 22,083 (figures from B. H. Pearce
Num. Chron., 5th series, XX).

Under the Empire the copper coins in three denomination
are important, whereas in silver the small denarius alone occurs
Copper coins are classed as 1st, 2nd and 3rd brasses (Aes I, II
III), according to size. In practice the standards varied a grea
deal, and as the years went by sizes diminished, till in the 3r
century 3rd brasses prevailed. But in theory 1st brass shoul
weigh 1 oz., and represent a sesterce (4 asses); 2nd brass a dupondius
2 asses; and 3rd brass 1 as (sometimes a semis, half as). Th
issue of these coins was left to the Senate, hence S.C. (*senatu
consulto*, at the Senate's discretion) on them, the emperors reservin
to themselves the issue of gold and silver. In early times 1st bras
are common, but towards the end the silver became so debase
that there was little need to distinguish it from the bronze coinage
Illustrations are given (Plate VIII) of ten 1st brass belonging to th
first two centuries, the majority of them representing emperors wh
had direct dealings with Britain; and of four 4th-century smal
gold coins. (N.B.—The *obverse* is the side with the head on it, th
reverse the other.)

1. Claudius (41 A.D.) TI, CLAVDIVS CAESAR AVG PM TR F
IMP PP Laureate head r. Rev. EX SC PP OB CIVES SERVATOS
in an oak wreath. (PM = Pontifex Maximus; TR P = tribunicia
potestate; PP = pater patriae; ob cives servatos = for the preserva
tion of the citizens.)

2. Nero (54–68). NERO CLAVD CAESAR AVG GER PM
TR P IMP PP. Laureate head r. Rev. ROMA—SC. Roma seated
to l. (Ger = Germanicus, for victories in Germany.)

3. Vespasian (71). IMP CAES VESPASIAN AVG TRP PP
COS III. Laureate head r. Rev. VICTORIA AVGVSTI—SC.
Victory to r. writing on a shield fixed to a palm tree, under which
Judaea seated and weeping. (Cos III = consul for the 3rd time
Conquest of Judaea.)

4. Domitian (85). IMP CAES DOMIT AVG GERM COS XI
CENS POT PP. Laureate bust r. Rev. ANNONA AVGVSTI—
SC. Ceres seated to l., with Abundance in front. (Cens. pot =
with censor's powers. Annona Augusti, the yearly supply of
provisions due to the Emperor.)

5. Trajan (104–110). IMP CAES NERVAE TRAIANO AVG
GER DAC PM TR P COS V PP. Laureate bust r. Rev. SPQR
OPTIMO PRINCIPI—SC in an oak wreath. (Dac = Dacianus,
for victory in Dacia. SPQR = Senatus Populusque Romanus.)

6. Hadrian (117–138). A rare coin. HADRIANVS AVGVSTVS.

Laureate bust, with cuirass r. Rev. FELICITATI AVG COS III PP. Ship with rowers and pilot going l. (Felicitati Aug = to the prosperity of the Emperor.)

7. Antoninus (153). ANTONINVS AVG PIVS PP TR P XVI. Laureate head r. Rev. COS IV SC. Mars to r. holding a spear and leaning on a shield.

8. Aurelius (162). IMP CAES M AVREL ANTONINVS AVG PM. Bust r. Rev. CONCORD AVGVSTOR TR P XVI COS III. Aurelius and Lucius Verus grasping hands. (Concordiae Augustorum, to the agreement of the Emperors.)

9. Commodus (186). A rare coin. M COMMODVS ANT P FELIX AVG BRIT. Laureate head r. Rev. PM TR P XI IMP VII COS V PP. Commodus seated l., holding a globe and crowned by a Victory flying behind him. (For a victory in Britain: (Ch. I, I).)

10. Septimius Severus (210). Rare coin. L SEPT SEVERVS PIVS AVG. Laureate head r. Rev. PM TR P XVIII COS III PP SC. Two Victories fixing a shield to a palm tree, at the foot of which are two captives. (This year the Emperor took the title of Britannicus Maximus for his victories over the Caledonians.)

11. Constantius Chlorus (292–304). Small gold: very rare. CONSTANTIVS NOB CAES. Laureate head r. Rev. HERCVLES CONS CAES. Hercules, nude, looking l., with club, 3 apples and lion skin. In exergue (bottom margin) SMAE. (Nob = nobilis; SMAE = sacra moneta, or mint, of Antioch, 5th workshop.)

12. Constantinus I (306–337). Small gold: very rare. CONSTANTINVS MAX AVG. Diademed bust r. Rev. CONSTANTINVS AVG. Victory marching l., holding crown and palm. In exergue CONS.

13. Valentinian I (364–375). Small gold. D N VALENTINIANVS P F. AVG. Diademed bust r. RESTITVTOR REIPVBLICAE. Emperor facing and holding a *labarum* (standard) and a Victory. In exergue TR. (D N = Dominus Noster; P F = Pius Felix, good and prosperous.)

14. Theodosius I (379–395). Small gold. DIV THEODOSIVS P F. AVG. Diademed bust r. CONCORDIA AVGGG. Rome seated facing, but looking r., holding shield on which is VOT X MVLT XV. In exergue CONOB. (Auggg. of the three emperors. Vot X, mult XV = vows made 10 times and renewed 15 times; CONOB—CON = mint of Constantinople; OB = obryzum, fine gold.)

Some Roman coins connected with the history of Britain, in

commemoration of victories gained there by emperors or their legates, are as follows: *Claudius*: Rev. triumphal arch, DE BRITANN (IS, over the Britons). *Hadrian* (122). Rev. ADVENTVI AVG BRITANNIAE (To the Emperor's arrival in Britain); and another with Rev.—female figure seated on a rock, with spear on arm and shield by side: BRITANNIA. From this and other similar figures the Britannia was taken for modern English coinage. *Commodus*. PIVS BRITANNICVS. Rev. an elegant winged Victory, naked to the waist, bearing a long palm branch in right hand and seated on a pile of shields. In exergue VICT(ORIA) BRIT(ANNICA), the victory in Britain. The reference is to victories of Ulpius Marcellus in Britain in 144 (Ch. I, H). An excellently executed coin. Similar coins of his sons *Caracalla* and *Geta*. The mints of *Carausius* and *Allectus* have been mentioned: their successors use the mark of the London mint.

SOME BOOKS

Agricola's Road into Scotland, Jessie Mothersole.

Antonine Wall, The, Sir G. Macdonald.

Archaeology in England and Wales, 1914–1931, Kendrick and Hawkes.

Archaeology of Roman Britain, R. G. Collingwood.

Auxilia of the Roman Imperial Army, G. L. Cheesman.

Berkshire, County Archaeologies, H. Peake.

Bignor Roman Villa, S. E. Winbolt and G. Herbert.

" Caerleon Amphitheatre ", in *Arch. Cambrensis*, by Tessa V. Wheeler.

County Archaeological Societies' Proceedings.

Gentleman's Magazine, 1731–1868, G. L. Gomme.

Huddersfield in Roman Times, I. A. Richmond.

Journal of Roman Studies: Sections on " Roman Britain ".

Londinium, Architecture and the Crafts, W. R. Lethaby.

Londinium, R. E. M. Wheeler's Report to Royal Commission on Ancient Monuments.

Prehistoric and Roman Wales, R. E. M. Wheeler.

Richborough, Kent: Report on Excavations, J. P. Bushe Fox.

Richborough, Guide to, by J. P. Bushe Fox.

Roman Art in Corinium, Remains of, Buckman and Newmarch.

Roman Britain and the English Settlements, Collingwood and Myres.

Roman Britain, British Museum Guide to.

Roman Britain, Buildings and Earthworks, John Ward.

Roman Britain, Everyday Life in, M. and C. H. B. Quennell, pictures.

Roman Britain, Map of, Ordnance Survey.

Roman Coins, H. Mattingly.

Roman Folkestone, S. E. Winbolt.

Roman London, The London Museum, R. E. M. Wheeler.

Roman Occupation of Britain, Haverfield and Macdonald.

Roman Provincial Administration, W. T. Arnold.

Roman Remains at Bath, A. J. Taylor.

Roman Roads in Britain, T. Codrington.

Romans in Cleveland, Frank Elgee.

Roman Theatre at Verulamium, A. W. G. Lowther.

Roman Wall, Handbook to, J. Collingwood Bruce, edited by R. G. Collingwood, 1933.

Roman York, Gordon Home.

Silchester Pottery, Thos. May.

Watling Street, With a Spade on, S. E. Winbolt.

Tacitus' Agricola, Furneaux and Anderson.

Terra Sigillata, Oswald and Pryce.

Verulamium, R. E. M. Wheeler.

Victoria County Histories, Roman sections.

Wroxeter, Fox's Guide to Reports on Excavations, J. P. Bushe Fox.

Yorkshire, County Archaeology, F. and H. Elgee.

SOME MUSEUMS WHICH EXHIBIT ROMAN-BRITISH SPECIMENS

Audley End Museum.
Aylesbury Museum.
Bangor University College, Welsh Museum.
Basingstoke Library and Museum.
Bath, Museum of Royal Lit. and Sc. Inst.   Roman Baths Museum.
Brading, I.o.W.   Roman Villa.
Brighton Public Library and Museum.
Bristol Museum.
Bury St. Edmunds, Moyses Hall.
Caerleon Museum.
Cambridge, Fitzwilliam Museum.   University Museum of Archaeology.
Canterbury, Royal Museum.
Cardiff, National Museum of Wales.
Carlisle, Tullie House Museum.
Carmarthen, Antiq. Soc. Museum.
Carnarvon Museum.
Chedworth, Roman Villa.
Chelmsford Museum.
Chester, Grosvenor Museum.
Chesters, nr. Chollerford, Northumb.
Chingford, Epping Forest Museum.
Cirencester, Corinium Museum.
Colchester Museum, Castle Branch.
Devizes Museum.
Doncaster Museum.
Dorchester (Dorset) Museum.
Dover Museum.
Durham, Cathedral Library Museum.
Eastbourne Museum.
Edinburgh, National Museum of Antiquities.
Exeter Hist. Museum, Rougemont House.
Falkirk, Dollar Park Museum.
Folkestone Museum.
Gloucester Museum.
Guildford, Museum of Surrey Archaeological Society.
Haslemere Museum.
Hereford Museum.
Hove Museum.
Huddersfield, Tolson Memorial Museum.
Hull, Mortimer Museum.
Ilkley Museum.
Ipswich Corporation Museum.
Kendal Museum.
Kettering Museum.
Lancaster Museum.
Leeds City Museum.
Leicester City Museum.
Letchworth Museum.
Lewes, Sussex Arch. Soc. Museum.

Lincoln Museum.
Littlehampton Museum.
London, British Museum.
         Cuming Museum.
         Guildhall Museum.
         London Museum, Lancaster House, St. James's.
Luton Museum.
Maidstone Museum.
Malton (Yorks) Museum.
Newark Museum.
Newcastle, Black Gate Museum.
Newbury Museum.
Newport (Mon.), Museum.
Northampton Central Museum.
Norwich Castle Museum.
Ospringe (Kent), Maison Dieu Museum.
Oxford, Ashmolean Museum.
Peterborough Museum.
Reading Museum, Silchester Collection.
Ribchester Museum.
Richborough (Kent) Museum.
Ripon Museum.
Rochester, Eastgate House Museum.
Rotherham, Templeborough Collection.
Saffron Walden Museum.
St. Albans (Herts), County Museum.
Salisbury Museum.
Scarborough Museum.
Sheffield, Weston Park Museum.
Shepton Mallet Museum.
Shrewsbury, Wroxeter Collection.
Southampton, Tudor House Museum.
Stockport Museum.
Sunderland Museum.
Taunton Castle Museum.
Thetford, Ancient House Museum.
Tunbridge Wells Museum, 6 Upper Grosvenor Road.
Warrington Museum.
Warwick, N.H.S. and Arch. Museum.
Wells Museum.
Whitby Museum.
Winchester Museum, The Square.
Worcester, Hastings Museum.
Worthing Museum.
Wrexham Museum, Holt R. Pottery Collection.
Wroxeter, Uriconium Museum.
Yeovil, Wyndham Museum.
York, Yorkshire Museum.

SOME ROMAN PLACE-NAMES, WITH ENGLISH EQUIVALENTS

Adurni, Portus	Portchester
Aelii Pons	Newcastle
Anderida	Pevensey
Aquae Sulis	Bath
Ariconium	Weston-under-Penyard
Atrebatum, Calleva	Silchester
Belgarum, Venta	Winchester
Branodunum	Brancaster
Camulodunum	Colchester
Clausentum	Bitterne
Corinium Dobunorum	Cirencester
Corstopitum	Corbridge
Dubris	Dover
Durnovaria	Dorchester, Dorset
Durobrivae	Castor, Northants.
Durobrivae	Rochester, Kent
Durovernum Cantiacorum	Canterbury
Eburacum	York
Gariannonum	Burgh Castle
Gessoriacum	Boulogne
Glevum	Gloucester
Icenorum, Venta.	Caistor by Norwich
Isca	Caerleon
Isca Dumnoniorum	Exeter
Isurium Brigantum	Aldborough
Lavatrae	Bowes
Lemanis	Lympne
Lindum	Lincoln
Londinium	London
Luguvallium	Carlisle
Othona	Bradwell
Pontes	Staines
Ratae Coritanorum	Leicester
Regnum	Chichester
Regulbium	Reculver
Rutupiae	Richborough
Segedunum	Wallsend
Silurum, Venta	Caerwent
Sorbiodunum	Old Sarum
Vectis Insula	Isle of Wight
Verterae	Brough
Viroconium Cornoviorum	Wroxeter

ROMAN EMPERORS

Augustus	B.C. ?–14 A.D.	
Tiberius	14–37	
Caligula	37–41	
Claudius	41–54	
Nero	54–68	
Galba	68–69	
Otho	69	
Vitellius	69	
Vespasianus	69–79	
Titus	79–81	
Domitianus	81–96	
Nerva	96–98	
Trajanus	98–117	
Hadrianus	117–138	
Antoninus Pius	138–161	
M. Aurelius	161–180	
L. Verus	161–169	
Commodus	180–192	
Pertinax	193	
Julianus	193	
Septimius Severus	193–211	
Caracalla	211–217	
Geta	211–212	
Macrinus	217–218	
Elagabalus	218–222	
Alexander Severus	222–235	
Maximinus	235–238	
Gordianus I	238	
Gordianus II	238	
Papienus Maximus	238	
Balbinus	238	
Gordianus III	238–244	
Philippus	244–249	
Decius	249–251	
Trebonianus Gallus	251–254	
Aemilianus	253	
Valerianus	253–260	
Gallienus	253–268	
Claudius II	268–270	
Aurelianus	270–275	

Tacitus	275–276
Florianus	276
Probus	276–282
Carus	282–283
Carinus	283–284
Numerianus	283–284
Diocletianus	284–305
Maximianus	286–305
Usurper, Carausius	286–293
Usurper, Allectus	293–296
Constantius Chlorus as	292–305
Constantius I	305–306
Galerius	305–311
Constantinus I:	
Caesar	306–312
Emp. W.	312–323
Emp. E. & W.	323–337
Licinius	307–323
Constantinus II	337–340
Constantinus III	337–361
Constans I	337–350
Julianus	361–363
Jovianus	363–364

West.

Valentinianus I	364–375
Gratianus	367–383
Valentinianus II	375–392
Theodosius I (W. & E.)	392–395
Honorius	395–423
Theodosius II (W. & E.)	423–425

East.

Valens	364–378
Theodosius I	378–395
Arcadius	395–408
Theodosius II	408–450

INDEX